Beyond Anger

Jennifer Minney

with illustrations by
Brian Minney

Silvertree Publishing

Published 2006
by
Silvertree Publishing
PO Box 2768, Yeovil, Somerset

ISBN: 0-9538446-7-6

A catalogue record for this book is available from the
British Library

Printed and bound by
Creeds the Printers, Broadoak, Bridport, Dorset DT6 5NL

Contents

1

INTRODUCTION AND OVERVIEW

HEALTHY ANGER

A Normal Human Emotion

Anger is a normal human emotion. And it is experienced by everyone, to varying degrees, every day of our lives. It is a natural and healthy response to wrong, injustice and pain, the feeling ranging from a fleeting mild annoyance to a deep and pervasive sense of outrage.

Anger has many different forms, and from ancient times these have been classified according to the cause, manifestation and intensity of feeling. Those that can be classed as normal include annoyance, frustration, irritation, indignation and rage. (Fury is often destructive, and bitterness and wrath always are, therefore do not come under this category.)

Annoyance, a word derived from the Latin, meaning 'hateful', is an angry response to molestation or harassment, whereas frustration is the feeling provoked when something hinders or prevents the reaching of a desired goal. The blockage can be a physical one, such as a personal injury or disability, a traffic jam, a computer crashing, or a malfunctioning piece of machinery. Or it can be emotional, like, for instance, a spouse not listening, a colleague misunderstanding, or a child refusing to obey. All of these produce stress, an inner tension that is hurtful – hence the anger. Similarly, irritation is a stress-related variation of anger, in this case induced by physical or emotional discomfort. A stronger form of anger is indignation, which is a scornful, more defiant response to wrong, injustice and pain, while rage is an intense, explosive reaction.

Many people have difficulty admitting to anger, even when it is mild or fleeting, because they confuse the feeling with destructive actions, like shouting or hitting. Not surprisingly, they want to avoid these behaviours because of the damage they cause, and because they can exacerbate the threat or harm that provoked the anger in the first place. But feelings are not actions. And anger, if recognised, acknowledged and channelled, can be used constructively, to bring about positive change.

A Powerful Form of Energy

Anger can be used to either build up or destroy because it is a very powerful form of energy. And, like any other form, such as electricity, is in itself neither right nor wrong. It depends, in part, on what you do with it. Electricity, for example, can be used to torture and even kill, although more usually it is safely harnessed to produce essential heat and light.

Anger can be considered useful and productive when it has a just cause, when the feeling aroused is in proportion to the cause, and when it is controlled and utilised to protect, preserve and enhance life. There are, in fact, times when it would be wrong not to be angry, such as when witnessing or hearing about child abuse, discrimination, or acts of hatred and violence. Every reform that ever took place in history occurred because someone was angry enough to do something: to prevent ill treatment, challenge injustice, alleviate pain and suffering, and improve the prevailing conditions.

A Drive to Life

Anger is both a normal human response to threat and a powerful form of energy because fundamentally it is a drive to life. Anger is about self-preservation and self-propulsion: an innate and instinctive urge to protect oneself, one's family and belongings, and to survive. This is why anger is naturally aroused when you, or those you love, are in physical or emotional danger. And it accounts for the tendency to lash out in frightening situations, to rage at injustice, demand vengeance, and defy chronic pain, determining that it will not keep you from living life to the full.

Anger as a drive to life is perhaps most forcefully demonstrated in an inherent need to grow and develop, to achieve one's aims and ambitions and realise one's full potential. When any of these goals are blocked, the resulting frustration is particularly strong. The word 'frustration' comes from the Latin *frustra*, meaning 'in vain'. But this sense of futility can create the compulsion to keep on trying until the blockage is removed and the difficulty overcome.

If you have a tendency to anger, you may not have realised that basically your feelings are normal and potentially useful, or that you have access to tremendous power that can bring about positive change in your own life and the lives of others. But before you can start using your anger constructively – or learn to channel it more effectively – you need, first of all, to acknowledge and accept its existence. Only then will you be able to recognise how you may be venting anger in harmful ways, identify your own typical patterns of misuse, and begin fully utilising, as God intended, this valuable and renewable source of psychic energy.

DESTRUCTIVE ANGER

Unrecognised Anger

Anger may be unrecognised because at some level it has been denied. Usually, this psychological defence comes into operation as a result of frightening childhood experiences. Constantly raised parental voices, harsh punishments or physical abuse will inevitably give rise to a fear of anger and a tendency to deny its existence in yourself. Similarly, if you have been brought up to believe that all anger is wrong, or if your parents hid their normal frustrations behind a smiling face, or disguised them as patient martyrdom, you may have convinced yourself that you never feel angry – hurt maybe, but not angry! Being put on a pedestal and having to live up to impossible standards, or being falsely seen as the black sheep of the family, will likewise create an unhealthy need to reject your shadow side and be seen as all sweetness and light.

Anger may also be unrecognised because it is repressed, that is, unknowingly pushed down into the unconscious. This usually happens after years of having to actively suppress it, when the habit of pushing it down becomes automatic. Your psyche takes over, rather like the body's automatic nervous system, acting instinctively and bypassing the mind when suddenly confronted with danger. Suppression, like denial, often begins in childhood, in families where it isn't safe to express angry feelings. This may be because a parent's anger is greater, especially if it is violent and uncontrolled, or because there is a constant fear of heavy-handed punishment or icy withdrawal. Children will also learn to sit on their anger if a parent is unable to cope with it and reacts immaturely: lashing out, verbally retaliating, or worse, breaking down crying and threatening to be ill.

When the suppression of anger turns to repression, there will inevitably be a build-up of this very powerful emotion, with a danger of its periodically bursting out. You will, of course, be very aware of any eruption – as will anyone else in the vicinity – but the underlying layers of stored anger are likely to remain hidden and unrecognised; they can only be discovered when you feel safe enough to begin looking beneath the surface.

Unexpressed Anger

When anger isn't recognised, it cannot be consciously expressed, hence the tendency for it to smoulder inside, like the molten rock in a dormant volcano, in danger of erupting when least expected and destroying everything in its path. But even when anger is noted and acknowledged, it might be kept submerged because of difficulty putting feelings into words, or fear of another's reaction. The fear may at times have a basis in reality, but it could also have been conditioned by past experience, in which case you will continue to stifle your anger when there is no longer any need to do so.

It requires trust to let someone know that you are feeling annoyed or irritated. And if, as a child, you were criticised and condemned for being angry, or teased and humiliated, you will probably anticipate the same response from everyone else and be anxious about showing any negative emotions. If you have experienced physical or sexual abuse, or been dominated and controlled by an autocratic parent, you may have developed such a fear of conflict or retaliatory action that any overt expression of anger will be virtually impossible. On the other hand, you might be suppressing anger because of a fear of your own actions if this very powerful form of energy were to get out of control.

When anger is persistently stifled, it can turn to bitterness. This is an unhealthy form of anger that eats away at your soul, damaging self-esteem, destroying happiness and ultimately revealing itself in a disgruntled and sour outlook on life. This keeps other people at bay, increasing any sense of grievance and creating yet more hurt and anger. So there is a downward spiral. Bitterness comes into being when grudges are nursed and wounds allowed to fester, because of an unwillingness to forgive.

Forgiveness does not mean denying, excusing or tolerating another's wrongdoing. Rather, it is a letting go of the need for revenge or restitution. But this takes time. Forgiveness is a process that involves working through the hurt and anger, writing off the debt and moving on. Being unable to forgive because you have not yet reached the stage of letting go, or because you don't know how to let go, is not the same as being unwilling to forgive. When anger is implacable and the natural impulse to remedy injustice turns to unyielding resentment, then it is essentially one's own self that is destroyed, not the person who first caused the wrong. And since it is impossible to keep unhealthy anger totally underground, others too are harmed, the innocent along with the guilty.

Uncontained Anger

Unexpressed anger does not stay safely contained; it leaks out like poisonous, bitter fumes seeping through cracks in a volcano's crust. Often it reveals itself in passive aggression, in which you attack others indirectly, and often unknowingly, through such things as backhanded compliments, subtle put-downs, cruel humour and sarcasm. Alternatively, you might inconvenience others, or sabotage their work, through chronic lateness, procrastination, or a persistent failure to pay debts or keep promises. Aggressive driving or accident proneness, that may put others as well as yourself at risk, are also indications of hidden rage. The fact that you can find rational explanations for your actions does not negate any underlying motive. Hurtful words and actions are always born of anger.

When anger is overtly expressed, but with little or no attempt to keep it within safe bounds, it is particularly devastating and can hurt yourself, other people and property. Self-harm might take the form of verbal assaults: putting yourself down, criticising, ridiculing or raging at yourself. Or the attacks may be physical. A tendency to starve yourself or binge eat is, among other things, a sign of erupting anger, as is self-mutilation – cutting, burning, head banging, or any masochistic act. The most destructive use of anger against oneself is suicide, unresolved rage being a major factor in depression.

When uncontained anger is directed at others, it can manifest itself in verbal threats, intimidating gestures, a tendency to snap, fly off the handle, or lash out in unprovoked fits of violence: pushing, hitting, kicking.... Often, such anger is displaced: vented on the wrong person. So anger with an abusing parent may be taken out on a child, and anger at a boss discharged onto a spouse. If anger goes back a long way and has been allowed to become all-consuming, it can turn to fury. This is a wild or passionate anger that is obsessed with thoughts of vengeance and punishment. Or it could develop into a cruel, implacable wrath. With both of these there is a compulsion to hurt and destroy, and the continuous strain of keeping the feeling in check will intensify the urge. The ultimate act of violence against others is, of course, homicide.

However, in order to avoid hurting others, you may, consciously or unconsciously, have learned to displace your anger onto property. Destroying your own creative works, such as paintings or poetry, could indicate frustration at yourself, but is more likely to be levelled at others, perhaps family members or friends who discouraged you, hindering creative expression; or magazine editors, publishers and the like who rejected your artistic endeavours. More obvious destructive behaviours, like smashing crockery, kicking doors, punching holes in walls, or acts of vandalism or arson, are also forms of displaced anger. Although the rage is vented on inanimate objects, it is actually directed at people, past or present, who have caused emotional or physical pain, and never been forgiven.

Whether your anger is repressed, directed at yourself, or vented on other people or property, it is important that you start recognising the extent of your anger and who you are really angry with. It is also important that you don't start berating yourself for any failure to identify your true feelings. You quite possibly had good reason at one time to keep your anger submerged. Children especially have to develop psychological defences in order to survive, because it is impossible for them to stand up to abusive or neglectful parents. Moreover, children who are ill treated tend to blame themselves. This propensity to false guilt is a major cause of anger turned inwards.

So, as you begin the process of gaining control over your anger, accept the angry part of yourself – not just the fact that you get angry – rather than condemning yourself. But while rejecting any false guilt, it is essential that you also start taking note of true guilt, which, like pain, is an indication that something is wrong and that you need to do something about it. Taking action now can prevent a lot of damage and heartache later on.

THE NEGATIVE EFFECTS OF ANGER

Self-Destruction

Anger, we have noted, is a form of energy. And when this energy is uncontrolled, the most damage inevitably occurs at the source, that is oneself. Whether or not anger is recognised, there are basically two ways of mishandling it: one is to clam up and the other is to blow up. And both are detrimental to one's physical, emotional and spiritual well-being.

If your tendency is to clam up, then the anger will seethe deep inside. You may not be fully aware of its existence, perhaps experiencing it as a sense of heaviness, or depression. Or it might manifest itself in psychosomatic symptoms – from the Greek *psyche* meaning 'soul' and *soma*, which means 'body'. These illnesses are sometimes dismissed as being 'all in the mind'. But psychosomatic illnesses are actual physical conditions that, if severe, do require medical intervention; it is their origins that are emotional. Diseases that can be caused or exacerbated by mismanaged anger include arthritis, gastro-intestinal problems, and some forms of cancer, as well as those associated with unrelieved stress.

With every surge of anger, whether held in or outwardly expressed, there is a typical physiological response: the fight or flight stress reaction. Several hormones, including adrenalin, are released into the blood stream, causing the heart to beat faster, and more blood to be diverted towards the brain and major muscle groups. At the same time, extra glucose is released from the liver, blood-clotting agents are increased – in anticipation of an injury – and lymphocytes, used to fight infection, are reduced. In other words, everything that is not needed in the crisis is temporarily shut down, while those parts of the body needed to deal with it are put into a state of high arousal. The stress reaction is meant to be short-lived. But when anger is constant, the body fails to return to its normal resting condition, remaining in a state of alert. And this can lead to a variety of illnesses, including hypertension, arteriosclerosis, stroke and heart disease, digestive disorders, thrombosis, circulatory problems, and increased susceptibility to infections. Anger can kill.

But far worse than the physical damage is the harm done to the soul, which the Bible defines as the seat of emotions and source of life and creativity. When anger is ongoing, the soul is starved of those positive nutrients, like love, beauty and truth, which it needs in order to thrive. And, little by little, this spring of life shrivels up and dies. The result is a feeling of emptiness, and increasing difficulty utilising and expressing creative gifts. The damage is compounded by the unavoidable build up of guilt and self-hatred – although these might be denied, or disguised by a couldn't-care-less attitude.

Since there is an overlap between psyche (soul) and *pneuma* (spirit), it is inevitable that, when anger is continuous or uncontrolled, spiritual development also is blocked. In the New Testament, the words for soul and spirit are sometimes used interchangeably, but the spirit, or 'breath' also has a higher meaning, referring to that part of a human that tends him or her towards God and enables communication with God. So, when the spirit is damaged, you inevitably become estranged from the cosmic flow of life, and from God himself. As a result, you are likely to feel cut off, disconnected, and alone. You will also feel socially isolated as you find it more and more difficult to relate to other people.

Severed Relationships

Whether your tendency is to clam up or blow up, anger damages relationships. People can sense anger, even when it is hidden, and their instinctive reaction is to keep their distance – emotionally if not physically. When anger is overtly expressed, through a propensity to argue, general hostility, or verbal or physical attacks, others will actively try to avoid you, unless their damaged self-esteem leads them to seek and remain with destructive partners. Uncontrolled anger leads to dysfunctional or broken marriages, short-lived friendships, and severed ties with family members, including children who may, as soon as they are old enough, cut off all contact in order to protect themselves from further harm. On the work front, repeated aggressive outbursts will alienate colleagues and superiors, interfere with concentration, and jeopardise your career.

However, in order to avoid being rejected, you might reject. In this case, your anger will cause you to break off relationships, or remain aloof, turning you into a loner or recluse. You may defiantly tell yourself that you don't need anyone, but inevitably your psychological and spiritual growth will be impaired. Development occurs in the context of relationships, where there is an interchange of thoughts and ideas and the receiving and giving of love. And this includes having a deep and loving connection with the environment.

Damaged Environment

We were made to interact, not only with other people, but also with the natural world. So if you are damaging the environment, you cannot live at peace with yourself. And conversely, if you are injuring yourself, you cannot live in harmony with your surroundings. The word 'ecology', which is the study of the environment, is derived from the Greek, *oikos*, which means 'house'; and a house is an extension of oneself. For this reason, anger that manifests itself in self-neglect is also likely to reveal itself in a lack of care for one's home, and a careless disregard of the planet. More overt anger is frequently displaced onto one's immediate surroundings; but where there is extensive

emotional damage, the anger is more widely dispersed, leading to attacks on animals, wilful desecration of trees and plants, the defacing of rocks, and the spoiling of the countryside.

Anger that spills over onto the wider environment is often linked with the false belief that humans have a right to take what they want from the world, regardless of the cost to plants and wildlife, and future generations. This blatant contempt for the needs of others, which might arise from an unconscious desire for revenge or restitution, is linked with greed. And it is greed that leads to deforestation, the tearing down of hedgerows and misuse of fields or marshland, oceans being over-fished, rivers and streams being polluted, and the ozone layer becoming irreparably damaged. Destructive anger leads, in the end, to a propensity to cause wrong, injustice and pain. And any ill treatment of creation leads to enmity with the Creator.

Enmity with God

When anger is consistently used in a harmful way, whether against oneself, other people, wildlife, or the natural world, then God cannot be your friend and ally. Although he is always ready to forgive, and to restore a right relationship, your unresolved anger will make it difficult for him to get close. Like a loving father trying to hold a toddler who is in the throes of a temper tantrum, he will be rebuffed and pushed away. But God is patient. He never forces us, but waits until we are ready to come to him and experience the love he is longing to bestow.

But maybe your anger has kept you from developing an awareness of spiritual values. Or, if you have been able to retain that innate sense of the eternal, you perhaps feel that you can't get through to God. You might even fear that he has turned his back on you because of *his* anger. God certainly does get angry. We are told that he is angry with the wicked every day.[1] He too is angry at wrong, injustice and pain. But God's anger is always just. And it is controlled – because God is in control. Unlike us, he doesn't become afraid when bad things happen, so he doesn't have a compulsion to lash out. Such is God's power that he can use evil for good. And ultimately, he will establish justice on earth, and bring lasting '*Shalom*': peace, harmony and well-being.

In the meantime, God doesn't want you to continue struggling with an anger problem. Rather, he wants you to bring it to him, so that he can help you regain control of your life and start connecting again with other people, the environment, and himself. But before you can learn to control yourself, you first have to know yourself. And this includes recognising your anger, knowing how it affects you, and how you generally manifest it.

RECOGNISING ANGER

Physical Signs and Symptoms

Everyone feels anger differently. And how it is experienced depends in part on one's personality; also on gender and age, the influence of hormones, and the weather. It also depends on the cause and extent of the anger and the form it takes. Remember, anger can be a mild annoyance, irritation or frustration, a burst of indignation, a seething rage or fury, bitterness, resentment, or violent, implacable wrath.

Although anger is an emotion, it is often first noticed in the body. And some of the symptoms – what you feel inside – will also be visible to others, who might notice the indications before you do. The most common symptom is muscle tension, in particular a knotted stomach, tight chest, stiff neck or headache; although you might experience anger as heartburn, nausea and indigestion. People can literally be a pain in the neck or make you sick! Alternatively, you might sense your heart pounding or fluttering, and feel out of breath. A dry mouth or an urgent need to urinate or defecate may also be symptomatic of anger.

More obvious signs include stiff posture, clenched hands, a habit of scowling or frowning, facial tics, flushing or trembling. Or perhaps you show anger mainly through your tone of voice, sounding brusque, belligerent or threatening, while your speech might be clipped or unnecessarily loud.

As you start tuning in to your body, and become more aware of your physical signs and symptoms, you will also find it easier to identify the initial feeling.

Emotional Signs and Symptoms

Like the physical pointers, the feeling of anger varies. For you, it might normally be experienced as an inner tension, so you feel like a coiled spring or an overstretched rubber band. On the other hand, you might sense a hard knot in the chest or stomach, a dull ache or heaviness. Anger may sweep over you in great surging waves, giving you a sensation of drowning, or it can feel like a red mist that blots out all other feelings, and even rational thought.

Sometimes, however, anger appears in another guise, the most common being depression. A major cause of recurring depression is repressed anger, so it is not surprising that anger itself can be felt as a general sadness, despondency, or even despair. Anger is also closely linked with fear, so it may be camouflaged as anxiety or a vague sense of unease. Unexpected bouts of nervousness sometimes have anger at their source, and persistent panic attacks may be hiding a deep sense of outrage.

Any of these emotional symptoms might also be visible to others, because of the vibes you give off. They will read your unconscious messages, such as, 'Keep away from me. I'm in a bad mood,' or 'I'm hurt and I don't want to talk to you.' And these will override any words or actions to the contrary. Also, through a psychological process known as projection, others can actually feel your feelings, which they might confuse with their own. They might sense your irritation or tension within themselves, or feel your waves of anger coming over them. When, however, you reveal your emotions more overtly, perhaps through a tendency to moodiness, fits of the sulks, manipulation or emotional blackmail, you are likely to stir up the other's anger, as you certainly will if you also act aggressively. Anger breeds anger.

Behavioural Signs and Symptoms

It is through behaviour that anger is most clearly revealed. And this includes speech as well as action. However, as with the emotional signs and symptoms, the anger may be disguised. For instance, statements like, "She makes me mad," or "I'm sick and tired of this place," invariably hide an underlying rage. The same is true of metaphorical expressions normally used to describe physical pain. Examples include: 'That really hit me hard', 'I can't stomach that', 'I'm feeling pretty battered', or 'I feel like I've been stabbed in the back'. In addition to these more obscure signals, anger can of course be very clearly demonstrated in speech, through threats, put-downs, insults and the like.

Anger that is revealed through your actions may also be disguised or blatantly obvious. For instance, anger turned inwards may be indicated through accident proneness: constantly tripping, falling off ladders, walking into things, and generally finding unconscious ways of injuring yourself. More overt self-harming behaviours include not only cutting, burning, etc., but also compulsive exposure to violence or pornography, eating disorders and misuse of drugs and alcohol. When aimed at others, anger can show itself passively, through non-cooperation or 'accidental' breakages or spillages; or actively, through withdrawal – the silent treatment – aggressive and unwanted tickling, teasing, or generally being annoying and aggravating. And anger is always at the root of physical attacks, sexual assaults or any act of violence.

Perhaps you have not, until now, been aware that your physical sensations, feelings, words or actions reveal anger. And if you have never associated anger with hurt, you may not have known that you have cause to be angry. Recognising what triggers your anger is the next step towards learning how to manage it. The causes can be divided into four major groups: global concerns, personal injury, your own self-angering thoughts, and deep-rooted unhealed wounds. With this last, you may have been left with a legacy of unresolved anger that will take time to process. So be patient with yourself as you set off on a journey that will take you beyond anger into a place of deep and lasting calm.

2

CAUSES OF ANGER

GLOBAL CONCERNS

Greater Exposure to Wrong

Nowadays, there is a heightened propensity to anger because we are exposed, as never before, to human sinfulness. We live in a 'global village': a world that has shrunk as travel and the exchange of information have become quicker and easier. So, just as in earlier times, people were affected by the happenings in their own village, we are impacted by events taking place on the other side of the world. And unfortunately, these are usually of a disturbing and worrying kind. Every day we hear or read about violence and crime, cruelty to children and animals, discrimination, political corruption, terrorist attacks and war; and these in addition to environmental disasters, some of which, directly or indirectly, are the result of man's greed or mismanagement. The anger these provoke is exacerbated by a sense of helplessness: we feel at times that there is nothing we can do to eradicate evil and right the world's wrongs.

Nearer to home, anger is aroused by the knowledge that we ourselves are at greater risk than ever before of becoming victims of crime, and that there is little we can do to protect ourselves or our families. Lawlessness prevails, in part because of the population explosion, with increased urbanisation and escalating unemployment. Overcrowding is in itself a threat because it contravenes our need for space; it makes us feel hemmed in and trapped, creating an urge to lash out, to make others back off or go away. And with the proliferation of large, impersonal businesses and political structures, we feel more and more that we are being controlled from afar by faceless bureaucrats. This erosion of personal autonomy triggers an instinctive urge to fight for our emotional, as well as our physical, survival.

In today's high-tech world, anger as a drive to life and emotional fulfilment is constantly provoked by the feeling of redundancy as machines and computers take over. And, with our throw away mentality, there is a general sense of impermanence. We feel devalued and easily dispensable, so we endlessly struggle to find some meaning and purpose in life: something that will be of lasting worth. Even those Judeo-Christian values that have stood firm for millennia have been eroded, and often in the name of sensitivity and caring. For some, this leads to confusion and disorientation; others are only too aware of the deception. Either way, there is a feeling of threat, which inevitably stirs up anger. And, as truth is turned on its head, as evil become good and good evil, the anger is intensified by a pervasive sense of injustice.

Increased Awareness of Injustice

There has, of course, always been injustice. But nowadays one cannot pick up a newspaper or watch a news programme without being stirred by the violation of human rights occurring somewhere or other in the world. We hear daily about racial and sexual inequality, unfair trading, exploitation of children, and oppression of the poor and needy, while evil people obtain power

and grow rich at others' expense. In our own country there are endless reports of school bullying, and of people being attacked or even killed because they don't happen to fit the accepted mould. And we hear *ad nauseam* about concern for the rights of criminals, who often evade justice, while the injured are given scant recognition. The anger provoked is partly altruistic, born of concern for the innocent victims. But it is also triggered by the threat to our innate sense of right and wrong, and the fear that next time, the casualties could be us.

Anger at injustice, like anger at corruption, is exacerbated by the persistent sense of danger, and lack of trust in the legal system to unfailingly protect the guiltless. To compound the problem, it is becoming increasingly more difficult in today's secular society to hold onto the belief that good will ultimately triumph. We inevitably become caught up in the social ethos, so our faith is undermined as we personally experience the erosion of individual and national identity, and the unfairness of having to conform to unjust laws and fit other people's ideas of what is acceptable. The inability of many to respect and appreciate differences has given rise to a lot of inner turmoil – and a lot of hurt.

Changing Experience of Pain

Pain, like wrong and injustice, has always existed; and in past eras people probably experienced far more physical pain than we generally do today. However, the social conditions and medical advances that, in more affluent nations, have reduced physical suffering, have also created a different attitude to pain. We no longer expect it. We see it as an intruder, something that gets in the way, ruining our plans and preventing us from getting on in life. So we want instant relief, and we endlessly search for some form of treatment or magic pill that will remove the hindrance. Because we repudiate pain, we no longer know how to cope with it, so it becomes frightening. And fear produces anger.

We are equally unable to deal with emotional pain, which is often condemned, or falsely viewed as a sign of weakness. These misperceptions lead to a tendency to deny or hide the pain, which partly accounts for the upsurge in emotional illnesses. The main causes, however, are linked to the erosion of personal identity, the disintegration of the family, and rejection of spiritual values. Most people today have known the hurt of being a cog in a machine, of having little or no sense of their own value; or the pain of being left standing while the world rushes on, too busy to listen and understand.

These new forms of emotional pain have affected every age group. As divorce becomes commonplace, more and more children feel betrayed, let down and angry; while even those with two loving parents, or youngsters who have been well supported through a family break-up, are affected by the spirit of anger that pervades many schools today. Adolescents have to cope not only with fluctuating moods due to hormone changes, but also with the struggle to find their place in a rapidly changing, uncertain world. And with the demise of the extended family, adults contend with new forms of loneliness, while they juggle, often single-handed, the increasing demands of work and children. The elderly too are experiencing new kinds of pain as they are no longer respected as in former days. Their long and varied experience of life is often discounted and their wisdom cast aside, while they are made to feel useless and a burden. In their case, the hurt is generally manifested as senility or depression.

Everyone has at some time known emotional and physical pain. And any injury to oneself naturally arouses anger, which will add to the outrage caused by today's zeitgeist. More usually, however, it is the other way round, and global concerns underlie and exacerbate the anger caused by personal experience of wrong, injustice and pain, making it much more difficult to manage.

PERSONAL INJURY

Being Wronged

In addition to the more general threats and danger that we experience in today's world, there are specific triggers that induce anger. These include anything that impairs our physical or emotional well-being. Being mugged or raped, for instance, will create a very powerful anger reaction; and because this is a response to wrong and injustice, as well as pain, the anger is likely to remain long after the physical injuries have healed. When the attacks are ongoing, as with spouse abuse, the anger too is continuous; although, in order to cope, it might be denied or repressed. Being on the receiving end of someone's passive aggression will also provoke anger, as will being wronged unintentionally. However, when another doesn't set out to harm, and the injury is minimal, the anger is usually fleeting.

In contrast, the anger aroused when a loved one is wronged can be very powerful and enduring, especially if it is a child or animal that is hurt. In these instances, it can feel as if you yourself have been assaulted. Similarly, you might experience intense anger if your property is wilfully damaged or your belongings stolen, not just because of the loss of valued possessions, but because the offences are a violation of your rights, indicating an unacceptable lack of care and respect for another human being. These crimes don't just damage material things; they also harm the soul.

Sometimes, however, it is the soul – the thinking, feeling part of the self – that is directly attacked. Examples include being constantly criticised or put down, derided, ridiculed, passed over, or made to feel stupid, unattractive, inadequate or inferior. Similarly, the soul can be injured through ongoing rejection or neglect, or through being made to feel that you are a burden or disappointment and not worth the other's time and attention. The anger comes, not only from the knowledge that you have been wrongly treated, but also from a recognition, at some level, that the other's perceptions are invalid, therefore unjust.

Being Misjudged

Being misjudged is very hurtful, and creates great outrage, because it is an attack on one's character. And it usually happens because someone has formed a wrong impression or misunderstood an action or motive. We all have an innate need to be recognised for who we are, so if we are falsely accused, or our motives misinterpreted, we naturally feel aggrieved. Children have a very strong sense of justice, hence their fury if they are reprimanded or punished unfairly, especially if a parent, on discovering the mistake, fails to acknowledge the error and apologise. If you were repeatedly misjudged as a child, you will probably have developed a hypersensitivity to injustice, resulting in a need to explain every action, or to always have the last word in an argument.

The need to put the record straight is particularly strong when one is misjudged as a result of slander or libel, or if there has been a gross miscarriage of justice, perhaps because of having been assessed on the basis of erroneous or biased information. If any of these have been your experience, or if for any reason you have been discriminated against, then you will have discovered that the anger is often manifested in a fight to restore your good name, and to reveal your true colours.

This innate sense of what is true and right will also lead to a determined pursuit of justice if someone you love has been treated unfairly, or been the victim of a crime. And only when justice has been done, or when there is an unshaken belief in God's righteous judgement, will emotional equilibrium be restored, and the pain that underlies the anger begin to ease.

Being in Pain

Wrong and injustice hurt, and the hurt leads to anger. But sometimes pain itself is the primary motivator. With physical pain, or a debilitating illness or disability, there is often a constant feeling of frustration because these afflictions get in the way: they keep you from moving freely, performing necessary tasks and achieving your goals and ambitions. If your pain is persistent or severe, you may have turned your anger inwards, causing you to rage at your own body for having let you down. Or the anger might be displaced, perhaps onto doctors, the social system, or even onto God.

When pain is a result of physical assault, your anger will understandably be directed at the perpetrator – unless it is denied or rationalised away. In this instance, the bodily suffering will act as a constant reminder of the wrong done to you: not only the physical harm, but also the invasion of your personal space. Anger will also be felt, but to a lesser degree, if the hurt was unintentional, such as when an injury is sustained as a result of someone's clumsiness or inattention. In this case, while you might forgive the person concerned, the pain will be a constant reminder, and might lead to periodic bursts of outrage.

Similarly, unremitting psychological pain will keep bringing the original cause to mind, leading to possible angry flare-ups. Soul-hurt is a normal response to any kind of emotional mistreatment, especially verbal abuse. But it is also a reaction to loss, whether through bereavement, divorce or separation; or loss of home, work, money or status. With all of these, the pain is experienced as grief, which is not just one feeling but a combination, which might include guilt, fear, sadness, yearning, emptiness, and anger.

How deeply grief is felt, and for how long, will depend on the closeness of the relationship or worth of the lost entity, as well as on your beliefs and values. The pain and anger will be greater if someone you regard highly is taken from you, or if something that means a lot to you is damaged or destroyed. These feelings usually recede with time, but they can be exacerbated or prolonged by your own thinking, especially if your perceptions are false and you exaggerate any wrong, injustice or pain. You might even see these afflictions where they don't actually exist.

SELF-ANGERING THOUGHTS

False Beliefs

Frequently, anger is triggered, not so much by the harmful experience itself, but by how it is interpreted. So the amount of anger is in proportion, not to the cause, but to an exaggerated sense of the injury, or of one's own importance. These false beliefs usually result from excessive hurt or overprotection in childhood, both of which create a vulnerability to any kind of emotional upset, and a habit of making mountains out of molehills. If, then, you believe that any kind of pain is intolerable, or that anyone who crosses you should be severely punished, the natural feeling of anger will be intensified. Moreover, these distorted views will create a propensity to mistrust, and may even lead to paranoia, with a compulsion to cut people off whenever you feel let down.

The erroneous belief that all your problems are everyone else's fault will also trigger or increase anger. And if you are unable to recognise your own contribution to any conflict, or how you might be setting yourself up to get hurt, then you will keep on repeating the same dysfunctional behaviours – and keep on getting hurt. Abdication of responsibility for your own feelings and actions is in effect an admission of powerlessness, which will inevitably heighten your anger as you impotently rail at other people, society, fate or God. It will also keep you from making those changes necessary to form healthy relationships, work effectively, and turn your fortunes around.

On the other hand, if, as a defence against feelings of helplessness, you develop a false belief in your own omnipotence and think that anything that goes wrong in your immediate vicinity is your fault, then you are going to feel permanently guilty and angry at yourself. This belief sometimes leads to obsessive-compulsive behaviour in which rituals are carried out to ward off the evil you fear you might cause. It can also trigger a conscious or unconscious need to punish yourself. Taken to an extreme, you might even feel guilty about world events that rationally you know have nothing to do with you. In this case, the feeling of self-condemnation will be very powerful, and, if you believe in God, you are likely to develop an unhealthy fear of his judgement.

With any false belief, the longer it persists, the more likely you are to see 'evidence' that proves you right, so reinforcing your view of yourself, the world and God. False beliefs and misperceptions go together.

Misperceptions

We tend to see what we want or expect to see. And if self-esteem has been damaged, there will be a propensity to view things in a false negative light, discerning rejection or hurt where they don't actually exist. You might, for example, perceive someone's failure to notice you as a deliberate snub, or convince yourself that your partner's preoccupation with personal concerns is proof that he or she no longer loves you. Assumptions about other people's thoughts and motives, without attempting to check them out, will inevitably create anger where there is little or no cause for anger.

You will also experience irrational anger if you see people as all bad, when perhaps there is only one aspect of their character that is annoying or irritating. This misperception often leads to a habit of labelling the person, rather than the behaviour. Examples include branding a woman who shouted at you as 'a horrible witch', or describing a man who acted insensitively as 'an unfeeling beast'. Such descriptions will naturally increase the initial anger their acts provoked, and make it harder to forgive.

On the other hand, you might view others through rose-tinted spectacles. This might seem a positive trait, but idealisation, like denial, is a psychological defence that protects you from something you are not yet equipped to deal with, in this case, human imperfection. So, when the defence is breached and you are confronted with the reality of human frailty, the result is a feeling of intense disappointment, fear, and again, unwarranted anger.

The tendency to see people as all bad or all good is akin to the inclination to generalise. For example, you conclude that no woman is to be trusted because one let you down, or all members of a particular race are evil because a small group perpetrated an atrocity. Similarly, you might transfer the negative attributes of one person onto another, who is actually quite different. Transference is a psychological phenomenon that also leads to misperceptions of God, perhaps seeing him as like an abusive earthly father or an autocratic church leader. Alternatively, you might have created an equally false, Father-Christmas-type God who will give you anything you want. Either way, your erroneous views will lead to a feeling of disappointment and outrage. Unrealistic expectations – of yourself, others or God – are bound to lead to unjustified anger, with greater difficulty controlling it.

Unrealistic Expectations

If you consistently expect too much of yourself, then you are setting yourself up to be stressed and angry – stress, we have noted, being a fight or flight reaction to any perceived threat or danger. Those most prone to stress are perfectionists and workaholics who are highly competitive, impatient, bad losers, and lacking the capacity to relax, play and have fun. This self-driven behaviour might be a search for love and acceptance, based on the false premise that these can only be gained through succeeding or winning. Or it could be a desire for power and control, used as a defence against feelings of weakness or inadequacy. Since this driven-ness is unrelenting and never satisfied, it constantly creates yet more anger, which perpetuates the behaviour. So there is a downward spiral.

An inordinate need for dominance is particularly damaging when it is linked with unrealistic expectations of others, especially when those others are children. If you have little or no understanding of child development and what can reasonably be expected at different ages, then you are likely to demand more of your children than they are able to give. You might even expect them to act like adults. So, when they inevitably fail to reach your impossible standards, you will feel frustrated and annoyed, and might want to vent your anger on them. But if their shortcomings lead you to view yourself as a failing parent, the anger will be turned in on yourself.

Insecurity about your own performance can also lead to, or be exacerbated by, unrealistic expectations of your peers. Lack of self-confidence is sometimes disguised as the false belief that you are always right, and that the world revolves around you, causing you to react with needless anger if others don't fit in with your plans or agree with your ideas and opinions. Fear and anger are very closely related, so you will also trigger unnecessary anger if you expect others to reject, disappoint or harm you; or if someone you thought would meet all your needs refuses to comply with your unreasonable demands, or proves to be all too human.

In the same way, anger is provoked when God himself doesn't fit a preconceived view and answer prayer in the way expected. God, unlike human beings, actually is perfect. So, knowing what is best for us, he doesn't always give us what we want. Moreover, God does not allow himself to be bribed or manipulated – just as he refuses to bribe or manipulate us. He does not intrude on our personal space, or coerce us into obeying the universal laws he has established for our own safety and well-being. Rather, he waits patiently for us to invite him in. And then, as a friend and guide, he assists our emotional and spiritual development, while his unfailing love acts as a healing balm for even the deepest wounds.

UNHEALED TRAUMA

Unmitigated Wrong

When anger is intense and all consuming, it is usually because of deep, unmitigated emotional trauma. The wounds may go right back to childhood, and if they were caused by wrong treatment, such as abandonment, neglect or abuse, then they need extra special care in order to heal. However, you may have prevented their healing through denying their existence or attempting to hide them. Perhaps you have told yourself that the wrongs were in the past, so no longer matter. But, as you may have already discovered, thoughts and feelings pushed into unconscious memory do not go away. They have a tendency to

31

reappear, or to break through in new destructive ways, especially if you have added to your wounds by continuing the wrongs and abusing or neglecting yourself: putting yourself down, criticising yourself, being overly harsh and self-punitive, or placing yourself in situations where you will be hurt all over again.

Wounds are also slow to heal, and the pain they cause unabating, if you have been the victim of a crime or been wronged by a trusted partner, friend or church worker from whom you legitimately expected better. In such cases, the trauma can be so great that it might seem impossible for any good to ever come of it. Spiritual abuse, which is the misuse of Scripture or one's position as religious leader in order to manipulate and control, is particularly devastating because it injures the spirit as well as the soul. It can leave you confused and bewildered, with your sense of self battered and your relationship with God in doubt. You are also likely to be consumed with false guilt and full of anger that you will probably turn in on yourself, not recognising where it really belongs.

With emotional or spiritual abuse, the harm done is often unintentional. And because of this you might not have realised that you are wounded, and so mistake the source of your pain and confusion. Or, you might have minimised the trauma because of a fear of surfacing anger getting out of control. Obviously, you will feel more angry as you become more aware of the wrong done to you. But when insight is allowed to occur naturally, the anger will only emerge at the rate your unconscious allows it. You might, however, need some form of assistance to minimise the pain, process the anger and use it constructively. The same applies if injustice has left you so badly traumatised that the wounds need expert care and attention.

Unresolved Sense of Injustice

Injustice, like wrong, is most likely to cause deep, pernicious wounds that don't easily heal when it is experienced in childhood, when the psyche is soft and impressionable. However, this plasticity of soul means that children are also resilient; they are not lastingly harmed by parents occasionally getting it wrong and accusing the wrong sibling of a misdemeanour. The damage comes from ongoing bias, favouritism, or unfair treatment. This last includes being repeatedly blamed for another's misbehaviour, or for a parent's unhappiness, or constantly being made to comply with impossible demands. If, for example, your parents always expected higher grades than you were able to achieve, or gave you responsibilities beyond your years, then the sense of injustice, along with a false perception of failure, is likely to persist.

Damage will also be extensive and enduring if you experienced a gross miscarriage of justice in adulthood. Unfortunately, it is often those who have the courage to stand up to wrongdoers who end up getting blamed. In the workplace, it is not unusual for whistleblowers to find, not only that they have been left to stand alone, but also that they are charged with being troublemakers. And those who voice their concerns about church leadership are frequently told that they are unspiritual, or that they have a rebellious spirit. These projections of guilt naturally cause deep hurt and outrage, as does being unfairly dismissed or expelled, or punished for a crime you didn't commit. In any of these instances, the pain will be immense, and the sense of injustice not easily resolved.

One cannot, of course, resolve injustice through putting the clock back: returning to an unhappy relationship, work situation or church in order to explain and put the record straight. It is, in fact, unwise to put yourself back in an abusive situation where you will be hurt all over again. And it is unlikely that you will receive an apology or compensation. You have to resolve the sense of injustice in your own mind. This involves recognising and acknowledging your own integrity, putting the guilt where it belongs, and working through the hurt and anger – as explained in Chapter 5 – so that the wounds can at last heal and the pain begin to ease.

Unabating Pain

Sometimes pain, whether physical or emotional, can seem unending; and when it continues with little or no sign of abating, it is very debilitating. With chronic physical pain there can be a permanent sense of frustration, which might be ignored, as one has at times to ignore the pain itself. On the other hand, the anger might be clearly evident as you constantly chafe at restrictions and perhaps rail at fate or God; or, when the pain is the result of physical assault, at the perpetrator. With an old injury that periodically flares up, or a progressive illness such as arthritis, there can also be a feeling that it isn't fair, and a compulsion to lash out, giving vent to a diffuse rage that has no specific object. The anger causes tension which increases the physical pain, causing yet more anger.

You might also be caught in a vicious spiral if emotional pain is ongoing, as for instance if you have to care for a disabled or chronically sick relative, or if someone you love is going off the rails, perhaps becoming addicted to drugs or alcohol. It hurts to see a loved one suffer, and it is frustrating, especially if there is little or nothing you can do to improve their situation. You are also likely to feel anger and resentment at any restrictions on your own life, and maybe false guilt for wanting time and space for yourself. Any tendency to self-condemnation will exacerbate the natural hurt and anger; and if your loved one actually dies, the pain can seem overwhelming.

The emotional trauma that is experienced with any kind of loss does in time recede. But if you are tormenting yourself with false recriminations, or if there have been unresolved hurts from the past, you can get stuck in the grief process. The pain also tends to be more persistent if there has been no possibility of saying goodbye, especially if your loved one was killed in a terrorist attack or natural disaster and the body never discovered. But any kind of unresolved ending, such as an acrimonious divorce or a child disappearing without trace, can leave you with wounds that don't easily heal, and a deep reservoir of anger that doesn't quickly dissipate.

However, with any kind of unhealed wound, there are steps you can take to reduce the pain, lessen the anger, and find healing and restoration. With lesser injuries it might be enough to talk through your feelings with a trusted friend. With deeper, more resistant wounds, professional help in the form of counselling or psychotherapy is indicated. It helps also to read about others who have found ways to resolve their problems and use their anger for good. The Bible is full of such examples, people just like us who learned, not only how to utilise the full range of human emotions, but also how to develop an inner sanctuary: a place of calm that remains undisturbed, however ruffled the surface.

3

EXAMPLES AND INSPIRATION

HOW OTHERS CAN HELP

Inspiring Hope

When anger dominates one's life, it is sometimes difficult to believe that the problem can ever be overcome. It helps, therefore, to discover that we are not alone, that even godly, well-respected people have struggled with anger, and yet been able to harness it, and use it for good. Such knowledge inspires hope, and it lessens the risk of getting bogged down in the mire of false guilt and self-condemnation. It also gives us somewhere to turn for guidance and direction. We learn best from example, although classes that teach anger management can of course be very useful, as can books like this one.

Our role models may be people we know – family members, friends, teachers, etc. Or they can be people we hear or read about. They may be living today, or they can be characters from history. Of this last group, perhaps our best source is the Bible. In both the Old and New Testaments there are stories of people just like us who got angry, sometimes excessively so, yet who found ways to channel their feelings in order to bring about positive change in their own lives, and the lives of others.

One such example is the Psalmist David. He often felt depressed and angry as he experienced misunderstanding, rejection, physical attack and exile. He was angry with his enemies, but more so with his rebellious children and treacherous friends. And he was outraged at political corruption and social injustice. David safely vented his feelings by writing poetry and music, while the sensitivity and spiritual insight that made him prone to depression and anger in the first place also enabled him to reach out to God, and find comfort and strength. And he used his anger constructively. It enabled him to survive the years of

36

exile in harsh desert surroundings, gain victory over his enemies, and later rule as king, wisely and justly.

Sarah, the wife of Abraham, is another example. Unable to produce an heir, she was probably angry at her own body, and maybe also with God. And her anger was inflamed by her maid, Hagar, who, according to the custom of the day, was bearing Abraham's child in her place. Hagar was insensitively flaunting her pregnancy, and treating her mistress with contempt. So, not surprisingly, Sarah's anger frequently spilled over. She coped by sharing her feelings with her husband, although it was not until she produced her own son, Isaac, and Hagar and her son left, that Sarah's anger finally diminished. When anger is constantly provoked, as Sarah's was, it can feel as if nothing will ever change, and the frustration and despair increase the anger. But nothing lasts for ever, and sometimes circumstances alter in sudden and unexpected ways.

Other examples include Moses, who was often angry at the constant griping and complaining of the people he was leading out of Egypt; while Nehemiah became frustrated with those who hindered the rebuilding of the wall of Jerusalem, following its destruction by the Babylonians. Jonah, already disgruntled at being sent to the heathen city of Nineveh, was angry enough to want to die when the only tree that provided any shade shrivelled up, exposing him to the burning desert sun. And the disciples of Jesus were not averse to squabbling amongst themselves about who would be the greatest. Yet all of these, in their different ways, learned to channel their anger and use it to overcome obstacles, endure hardships, confront evildoers, and bring healing and hope to those in need. But first, they had to learn to control it.

Teaching Control

As well as providing inspiration and encouragement, people who have learned to master their anger also teach us how to develop self-control. Normally, the first people we learn from are our parents. But unfortunately, many caregivers are unable to keep their own anger in check, so are incapable of containing their children's. This makes the little ones feel unsafe with their own aggressive feelings, creating the need to build defences, such as denial or repression. But it is never too late to start taking down the defences, acknowledge the anger, and learn how to harness it. Here again, positive role models may be our own friends and acquaintances, or characters from history.

In the Old Testament we have a wonderful example in Jacob, the son of Isaac and grandson of Abraham and Sarah. Jacob went through life with a chip on his shoulder, feeling that he was hard done by: as the second-born twin, he lived in his brother Esau's shadow. His resentment and desire to get one up on his brother led to estrangement and heartache for all the family. But, over time, he learned to master his anger. And he directed this powerful form of energy into winning a beloved wife, Rachel, increasing his livestock and providing for his large family. Jacob prospered and eventually became reconciled with Esau, while his name, meaning 'trickster', was changed to Israel – 'a prince'. Jacob's battle with anger was a lifelong one. But at least he didn't take it to the grave with him, unlike others who act as a warning, showing what can happen if, instead of controlling anger, anger is allowed to control us.

Acting as a Warning

The first biblical record of the destructiveness of uncontrolled anger is the story of Cain and Abel – sons of Adam and Eve. Cain was furious because God had accepted Abel's offering and not his, and in an unguarded moment he lashed out, killing his brother. As a result he became an outcast, cut off not only from his family, but also from his own self.

Whenever we hurt others – homicide being the ultimate harm – something dies within us, and we ourselves are destroyed. This is also what happened to Saul, the first king of Israel. He came from a wealthy, powerful family, and was himself impressive. And he started out well. But his lack of faith in himself and God set him on a downward path to destruction. His insane jealousy of David, who was later to replace him, led Saul to deprive the youth of his rightful honours, make an attempt on his life, and ultimately banish him. But while David prospered, Saul became increasingly a prey to his own uncontrolled rages. He died after falling on his own sword, having been severely wounded in battle.

Anger, as Saul discovered, is extremely potent, and when we don't learn to handle it can be very frightening – like being behind the wheel of a very powerful car when we haven't yet learned to drive. Anger is a potentially lethal weapon, but equally it can take us to places we never dreamed of. We will look now in more detail at three Bible characters who learned to use their anger constructively. The first of these is Elihu, generally considered to be the first angry young man.

THE FIRST ANGRY YOUNG MAN

Elihu's Beliefs and Values

Elihu was one of Job's comforters, appearing in the ancient poem that explores the puzzling question of why bad things happen to good people. Job was a moral, upright man, and very rich, his wealth comprising large herds of donkeys, oxen, sheep and camels. But in a series of catastrophes these were all wiped out, after which a whirlwind killed his entire family of seven sons and three daughters who were gathered in the home of the eldest. Finally, Job developed painful boils, probably a psychosomatic disorder brought on by extreme stress; and, in despair, his wife angrily told him to curse God and die. The term, 'Job's comforter', has come to mean someone who is little help in time of trouble. But Job's friends, unlike his wife, were at first very supportive. Three of them, older men, set off immediately to be with Job, and they were so shocked by his changed appearance that they sat down and wept with him, sharing his grief. Elihu, a younger man, joined them later.

When Job finally spoke, after seven days, he cursed the day he was born. Then the three older men tried to help him make sense of his calamities, while Elihu, out of respect for his elders, said nothing. But as he listened to their long-winded discourses he became more and more incensed. He was angry with the three comforters because of their dogmatic assertions that all suffering must be the result of personal sin, and with Job for his arrogant justification of himself, even making himself out to be more moral than God. Elihu had a deep reverence for God and, unlike the others, viewed him not only as a judge, but also as a teacher who uses suffering to form character. In the end, he could contain his thoughts and feelings no longer: they were, he said, like wine that has no vent and was about to burst the container.

Elihu's Indignation

Although Elihu's anger had been building up for some time, he began his argument by calmly expressing his regard for the older men, his sincerity and devotion to God, and respect for God's revelations which, he reminded them, came to the young as well as the old. He then rebuked Job for his self-righteousness, and for asserting that there is no point in being moral. And he confronted the three friends with their inconsistency: they had no answer for Job's suffering and yet had condemned him. He argued that God is greater than men, and that unlike us he knows everything, and always acts justly.

Then, in spite of his burning indignation, Elihu was able to give Job space to respond. When he kept silent, Elihu continued, refuting Job's argument that there is no advantage in serving and delighting in God, and berating him for having the audacity to accuse God of being hostile towards him. He reproached Job for his rebelliousness and petty focus on what God should be doing for him, and went on to expound on the greatness of God as revealed in nature, and the smallness of man in comparison. He concluded that, in view of our limitations, we should lean on God, and not on our own intelligence.

Elihu's Vindication

At this point God intervened, speaking from a whirlwind. God seemingly took up Elihu's argument, pointing out the wonders of creation – the vastness of the sky and ocean, the power of thunder and lightning, the treasures of the snow, the mystery of birth and death.... And God asked Job where he was when the world came into being and the stars sang together. He questioned whether Job was able to understand the behaviours of sea creatures, animals and birds, or control the wind and rain. And he accused Job of darkening counsel through words without knowledge. But God was also angry with the three older friends for accusing Job, and for not speaking what was right. Against Elihu God had no charge.

Elihu's views, like those of the three other comforters, were also rather simplistic; but, unlike the others, he acknowledged his limitations, accepting that we can give no definitive answers to the puzzling question of human suffering. It was perhaps his humility that enabled Elihu to keep his anger under control, and use it to confront older men who at first had intimidated him, making it hard for him to speak. Also, Elihu's anger had a legitimate cause.

Anger, you will recall, is a response to wrong, injustice and pain. And Elihu was seething because of the wrongness and injustice of the older men's arguments and Job's accusations against God. And he was enraged at Job's devastating afflictions. He had every reason to be angry. But he kept his anger in proportion to the cause. He did not lash out, get violent, or throw a tantrum. His behaviour for one so young was, in fact, very mature. And one can assume that, following God's intervention and the repentance of the four, Elihu's anger dissipated. However, the next person we are going to look at experienced a very different kind of anger, and wasn't able to get rid of it quite so easily.

CALL ME 'BITTER'

Naomi's Losses

Naomi, whose name means 'pleasant', lived at the time of the Judges, about the middle of the 12th century BC. It was a period of wars, intrigues and rivalries, although the story of Naomi and her daughter-in-law, Ruth, is set in a peaceful country idyll. However, the story begins with a famine, which caused Naomi, with her husband, Elimelech, and her two sons, to leave their home town of Bethlehem for the land of Moab, about fifty miles away. They stayed there for about ten years, during which time her two sons married local Moabite girls, Ruth and Orpah. Then Elimelech died, leaving Naomi a widow. And shortly after, her two sons also died.

Eventually, Naomi heard that the famine in Bethlehem was over, and she decided to return to her own country. Her two daughters-in-law accompanied her part of the way, where she urged them to go back to their own mothers. She lamented bitterly that she was too old to have another husband and children. And even if she could, would they wait for the boys to grow up! Orpah, persuaded by the sense of this argument, elected to turn back. So, after kissing her mother-in-law goodbye, she headed off home. But Ruth insisted on staying, with the immortal words, "Where you go I will go, and where you stay I will stay. Your people will be my people and your God my God. Where you die I will die, and there I will be buried." [2]

After a long and hazardous journey the two women reached Bethlehem, and the whole town was stirred. Some of Naomi's old friends exclaimed, "Can this be Naomi?" But she told them not to call her Naomi any more, but Mara, which means 'bitter', because, she said, God had dealt bitterly with her. She had gone away full and come back empty.

Naomi's Bitterness

Following her losses, Naomi was experiencing a typical grief reaction. Sometimes the various feelings that comprise grief – sadness, yearning, fear, anger, etc. – are felt one at a time; at others they are all mixed up together. And it would seem that, during this phase of her grief, Naomi's anger was uppermost. She was obviously angry with God, and possibly also with her husband for having taken them to Moab in the first place – and for having died. And she was probably angry with her sons, Mahlon and Chilion, for having lived up to their names, meaning respectively, 'weak' and 'pining'. To experience three bereavements in such short succession would have made Naomi's grief seem overwhelming. And had it not been for the kindness of Ruth and Orpah, she might have gone under. It is not surprising then, that her anger had turned to bitterness.

And yet, Naomi did not allow the bitterness to sour her completely. Although she was hurt, confused and angry, she continued to live up to her given name, and remained pleasant. She could not otherwise have inspired such continuing love and devotion in her daughters-in-law, especially in the one who chose to remain with her.

Naomi's Restoration

Naomi and Ruth arrived in Bethlehem at the time of the barley harvest. Long before, Moses had established a law, giving the poor the right to glean after the harvest. So, at Naomi's suggestion, Ruth went to follow the reapers. She came home with far more than expected, and when Naomi discovered that Ruth had been working in the fields of Boaz, a near kinsman, she experienced a stirring of hope. Throughout the barley and then the wheat harvest, the reapers, at their master's bidding, deliberately left handfuls behind for Ruth to gather. And Naomi, with renewed trust in God, told Ruth to put off her mourning and spend the night sleeping at the feet of Boaz, on the threshing floor. This was an old country custom, carried out in order to remind the next of kin of his duty of producing heirs for a deceased relative. Naomi had prior right to this claim, but she was standing aside for the younger woman.

Ruth carried out her mother-in-law's instructions, and Boaz, waking in the night, told her that there was a nearer relative. But, he assured her, if this other kinsman was not willing to redeem – buy back – the field Naomi had been forced to sell, and marry Ruth to continue the family name, then he would do all that was necessary. When the other relative declined, Boaz married Ruth, and she produced a son, Obed, for the dead Mahlon, making him Naomi's grandson.

Naomi could have allowed her bitterness to take over and turn her into a sad and lonely old woman, living out her days in a foreign country, abandoned and forgotten. Instead, her grief and anger, along with her love for her daughter-in-law, motivated her to make the long and dangerous journey back to Bethlehem, and to set about turning evil to good. And her actions produced far more good than she could ever have imagined: Obed was the grandfather of King David, who was a direct ancestor of Jesus.

Jesus, of course, is the perfect example of how to manage anger. He was often angry at wrong, injustice and pain, and he expressed it in no uncertain terms. His anger was not different in kind to ours. It was righteous because it had a valid cause, it was in proportion to the cause, and it was put to good use, to fulfil a moral purpose. Through his example his disciples learned to discipline themselves, and vent their anger safely and designedly. And it is one of these whom we will consider next: the apostle John. Like Naomi, he discovered that when anger is mixed with love it can achieve wonderful things.

THE SON OF THUNDER

John's Calling

John grew up in Capernaum, on the north west shore of the Sea of Galilee, where his father, Zebedee, ran a successful fishing business. His family was a wealthy one, able to employ servants, and to help provide for Jesus' needs during his three-year ministry. It is thought that John and his brother James were cousins of Jesus, their mother, Salome, being Mary's sister.[3, 4, 5] If this is so, then Jesus would have known John from childhood.

But it was when Jesus began his ministry at the age of thirty, and called the two brothers from their fishing to become 'fishers of men', that we first get to know them.

James and John, along with Andrew and Peter, were the first disciples Jesus called. And by the time he had chosen all twelve, he had nicknamed the two brothers '*Boanerges*', meaning 'sons of thunder'. This is probably because they were zealous, high-spirited and outspoken Galileans; but perhaps also because their ardour for God was sometimes unchannelled, and they tended to react angrily whenever they were crossed.

John's Misdirected Zeal

John, who was probably the younger brother, had a propensity to speak without thinking, and to express his anger aggressively. This was shown when a Samaritan village refused to provide them with the customary hospitality. The brothers immediately flared up, wanting to call down fire from heaven to destroy the village and wipe its inhabitants off the earth. Jesus rebuked their misguided zeal, and their lack of true insight into what his ministry was really about.

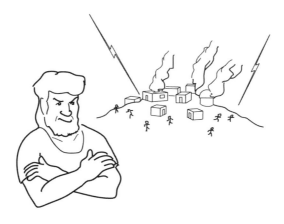

On another occasion the two brothers annoyed the other disciples by asking Jesus if they could sit on either side of him when he came into his kingdom. The other disciples also wanted these honoured positions but, unlike James and John, hadn't the gall to request it, instead quarrelling amongst themselves. When Jesus responded by asking the brothers if they could drink the cup that he was going to drink, they thoughtlessly and confidently asserted that they could, which probably annoyed the other disciples even more.

However, in spite of their arrogance, their selfish ambitions and angry call for revenge when they were slighted by the Samaritans, the brothers, along with Peter, were given special privileges. They were the only disciples present when Jesus raised Jairus' daughter from the dead, and the only ones allowed to accompany him up the mountain of transfiguration, where they witnessed his eternal glory. John and Peter were the two chosen to prepare for the last supper, and the three were elected to be with Jesus in the Garden of Gethsemane, to support him in those agonising hours before his crucifixion.

John is almost certainly the disciple described as the one whom Jesus loved, mentioned in the fourth Gospel. This version of the life of Jesus differs considerably from the others: while Matthew, Mark and Luke give a factual account, John's is more reflective and poetical, revealing his creative flair and deep sense of the spiritual. These attributes often go with anger because people who are more in touch with eternal values are more likely to feel outrage when they witness wrong, injustice and pain – it is only those who don't care who never get angry. But equally, creative people who are sensitive to God's leadings have the very qualities needed to channel their anger, and use it for good.

John's Transformation

It was probably John's creative and spiritual potential that drew Jesus to him in the first place. And, as John learned from Christ's example, basking in the light of his care and compassion, the Son of Thunder was transformed into the Apostle of Love. So it was to John that Jesus entrusted the care of his mother, Mary, as he was dying on the cross. And after his resurrection, which John was one of the first to witness, this uneducated fisherman truly became a fisher of men, astounding the Jews with his learning and boldness of speech and action. He was driven now, not by a craving for revenge, but by a desire to see people saved and healed: for love to triumph over evil as he had seen it triumph in his risen Lord and Saviour. And such was his impact that the religious authorities of the day accused him and the other disciples of turning the world upside down.

By the time the apostle Paul visited the Jerusalem church, years later, John had become a highly respected leader, and his untiring message was, "Little children, love one another." This theme is evident in his gospel, throughout which he stresses the importance of our relationship with God and the need to abide in Christ's love. Similarly, his letters are full of exhortations to love one other as God has loved us, and he reminds us that the mark of a true Christian is one who has learned to love. According to the early Christian writers, Irenaeus and Jerome, in his old age John had to be carried to meetings where he would repeat, "Little children, love one another."

Yet John's development from Son of Thunder to Apostle of Love did not turn him into a weakling. On the contrary, he never lost his anger, but channelled this powerful form of energy and drive to life so that many, including himself, could experience life in all its fullness, as Jesus had promised. John had discovered that true power does not come from lashing out, or threatening vengeance and retribution. These are actually signs of weakness, indicating fear and insecurity and an inability to control oneself. True power is love in action. It is the courage to stand up for the right, to deal justly, and to soothe fears, comfort those who mourn, bind up their wounds and heal the broken hearted.

Ultimately, it is love that enables us to move beyond anger into a place of calm. But this, as John and other Bible characters discovered, is a lifetime's work. The first priority, which we will now discuss, is to learn how to manage anger, keeping it from getting out of control. You can do this through becoming more aware of the signs and symptoms, finding appropriate ways of expressing anger, and acquiring some coping skills, such as how to be assertive, how to deal with conflict and, above all, how to relax.

4

MANAGING ANGER

INCREASE AWARENESS

Acknowledge the Existence of Anger

In order to manage anger, you first have to accept its existence. If this is difficult for you, begin by reminding yourself that anger is a normal, healthy emotion, as well as a useful and powerful form of energy, and a drive to life. The Bible tells us not to sin in our anger; [6] that is, we must not use it destructively, in ways that harm ourselves, other people or property. Rather, we should use it for good, as Jesus did. His anger was especially aroused by hypocrisy and the show of religion, without any real care for people's needs. He was more concerned with spiritual and emotional development than with keeping man-made laws – which he frequently broke.

In order to fully develop as human beings we have to accept and utilise the full range of God-given emotions. When we don't, it's like playing a musical instrument using only the top notes, or painting a picture with only bright or pastel shades. We need our shadow side. So, rather than denying or rejecting the angry part of yourself, turn it to advantage, to bring into focus and accentuate your gentler, more loving aspects. There will, of course, be times when you get it wrong. But, rather than condemning yourself, learn from your mistakes, forgive yourself, and move on. And encourage yourself with the thought that the more comfortable you feel with anger, and the quicker you can recognise it, the easier it will be to manage.

Notice the Signs and Symptoms

Often, those who have difficulty controlling their anger don't realise until too late that they *are* angry. It is essential, therefore, that you learn to recognise the signs and symptoms. First, think about any chronic or recurring physical problem, such as back pain, headaches, or diarrhoea. These might be psychosomatic and caused or exacerbated by repressed anger. Then, on a day to day basis, practice tuning into your body, noting any minute changes. Do you, for example, develop a dry mouth when you are angry, a knotted stomach or pounding heart, or experience nausea, indigestion, shaking or trembling? And what about your body language? Are you signalling anger through clenched hands, stiff posture, scowling expression, brusque speech or a raised voice?

While you are familiarising yourself with the physical signs and symptoms, also take note of the feelings. Do you, for example, experience anger as a general tension, a knot of pain, a dull, heavy weight, surging waves, a red mist...? Or is your anger disguised or concealed by other emotions, such as hurt, fear or depression? With practice, you will become more adept at noticing the first indications of anger, making it less likely that you will start acting it out.

When anger is manifested in behaviours, it is usually too late – you have already lost control. Nevertheless, it helps to monitor your actions, and especially to be on the alert for hidden anger, as in aggressive driving, unnecessary risk taking, accident prone-ness, or constant lateness, forgetfulness or procrastination. Also recognise anger in your words: in statements like, "She's a pain in the neck," "I'm fed up," or "I've had it up to here." And whether your anger is overt or hidden, active or passive, turned inwards or directed at others, ask yourself who or what you are angry with, and why.

Identify the Causes

If you are constantly angry, you could be affected more than you realise by events taking place worldwide. So observe your reactions when you are watching news programmes or documentaries, and question whether you are exposing yourself to far more violence than is good for you. Also, consider your values, and develop a greater awareness of those issues most likely to cause outrage. Is it, for example, global warming, deforestation, terrorism, or exploitation of children? Or do you get hot under the collar about politics or social attitudes?

While questioning your global or social concerns, also think about unresolved personal issues. Have you been greatly wronged, suffered a gross injustice, or been so badly hurt that you have a deep well of unprocessed rage? Any unhealed wounds from the past will leave you scarred and vulnerable to present-day distress, making it much harder to deal with.

Even if anger is deep-rooted, it is usually triggered by current situations and events, some of which might seem so minor or unimportant that you habitually disregard them, not recognising the effect they are having on you. It is important, therefore, that you start taking note of any wrong, injustice or pain you are experiencing right now. Are you, for instance, being overlooked at work, or exposed to rude or obnoxious customers? Are you being ill treated by a spouse or partner, does a friend keep letting you down, or are you tearing your hair out over unruly and disobedient children? Perhaps you don't handle frustrations well, things like constant interruptions or difficulty getting hold of vital information? Or do you have a chronic physical condition that holds you back from doing the things you want to do, making you angry with yourself, or perhaps the Health or Social Services, fate, or even God?

While contemplating any current triggers, bear in mind that

there are times when one can feel angry and not know why. In this case, mentally go over the events of the day. It may have been something quite trivial that upset and angered you: a look, a harsh or insensitive word, or a build-up of small annoyances that you failed to register. Or it could have been something you experienced only at an unconscious level, like someone's aggressive or rejecting body language. But then you might simply be having an off-day, as everyone does, perhaps because you're tired or not feeling well; or, for women, because it's the wrong time of the month. In these instances, you will probably over-react to the smallest of irritations. However, if you constantly feel more angry than the situation warrants, you will need to work especially hard at recognising your over-reactions and understanding why these occur.

Recognise Over-Reactions

Whenever you are angry, ask yourself if the anger is in proportion to the cause. If it is excessive, then take time to reflect on this, and see if you can identify other related sources. If, for example, you feel inordinate hurt and rage whenever someone lets you down, perhaps the sense of betrayal latches onto unresolved childhood experiences of neglect, and a deep-rooted fear of abandonment. If you tend to go ballistic whenever a child spills a drink, making a mess on the carpet, maybe your anger is mainly directed at a parent who messed up your life. Children often trigger disproportionate anger, especially if you see a disliked part of yourself in the child.

But perhaps you over-react, not so much because of unresolved issues from your childhood, but because of your own thinking. If you care too much about other people's opinions, exaggerate the importance of others' words or actions, or think that any pain or upset is intolerable, then you are setting yourself up to feel unnecessary anger. So begin questioning your thinking, taking especial note of any emotionally-charged language, like, "I must have...", or "It's not fair. That shouldn't have happened to me." And remind yourself that life often isn't fair, and frustrations happen to everyone. You are not being singled out for unjust treatment.

In order to begin changing false beliefs, it might help to think about the ABC of anger. It is not A – the Activator – that leads to C – the Consequence – but B – your Belief. So, for example, it is not your husband coming home late that makes you angry, but your belief that he is inconsiderate and uncaring. And it is not a friend forgetting your birthday that leads to anger, but your belief that she doesn't think you important. Anger, like stress, is often self-induced. But as you increase your awareness of just and unjust anger, and begin recognising any causes, you will find it easier to respond appropriately, and to express your anger more constructively.

EXPRESS ANGER APPROPRIATELY

Challenge Faulty Thinking

It is not enough to merely recognise faulty thinking patterns; you also have to challenge them. And it is easier to do this when you are not feeling angry. Begin by giving yourself time to reflect on your beliefs – about yourself, other people and God. Do you, for example, tell yourself that you are inferior or a failure, or think that everyone, including God, is out to get you? Do you think that all your problems are everyone else's fault, or blame yourself for everything that goes wrong in the family, or even in the world? As you identify your false beliefs and their origins, then start refuting them. This includes any valid beliefs you may have had as a child that are no longer relevant. For instance, if a parent abandoned you, it doesn't follow that your partner will; and because a parent didn't love you, it doesn't mean that no one else can.

While challenging your belief system, also question any misperceptions. Do you, for instance, see hurt and rejection where they don't exist, have a tendency to generalise, or have a lopsided view of others, either seeing them as all bad, with no redeeming features, or so perfect that any indication of human frailty comes as a shock? As with false beliefs, it is easier to identify and correct any distorted vision when you are in a settled frame of mind. But also practice challenging your views the moment someone angers you. If, for instance, a friend lets you down, note your disgruntled and negative thoughts, silence them, and consider other possible explanations for his or her behaviour.

As you work at correcting your faulty perceptions of others, also look at your expectations. Are you demanding too much of people, or contemptuously writing them off as a waste of space? These questions are especially important if you consistently ask too much of your children, creating a downward spiral of let-down, frustration, and yet more failure on your children's part. You can reverse this particular trend, first by examining it, then by finding out what you can reasonably hope for at different ages. There are books in the library that will provide you with the information you need, or you might want to attend a parenting class. Meanwhile, also challenge and begin to change, through acquiring some sound biblical knowledge, any unrealistic expectations of God. Discover what a good Father is like, and denounce those internalised parental voices that keep you trying to live up to impossible standards. Start recognising your true worth, and give yourself permission to do things in your own time and your own way. This includes learning how to manage anger, and using those controls that work best for you.

Practice Controls

Anger control begins in the mind. So, when you are feeling calm and relaxed, think about the kinds of things that make you angry, and your usual reaction. Then imagine yourself responding differently. If you are easily frustrated, see yourself walking away from a tense situation, making a cup of tea, giving yourself space, and returning to the obstacle with a clear mind. Or picture yourself in a traffic jam, using the time to unwind: listening to music, or amusing yourself mentally writing poetry or short stories. If you have difficulty handling other people's anger, then mentally rehearse a conflict situation, visualising yourself standing firm and unshaken. And, bearing in mind that 'a soft answer turns away wrath',[7] think about what you might say, and how you might say it. Then, start putting your new thoughts into practice, beginning with those closest to you, whom you find the least threatening.

If you have frequent arguments with a spouse or partner, you might find the Time-out Technique helpful. Choose a time when you are both in a good mood, and make an agreement that, whenever an altercation starts getting out of hand and one of you calls "Time out," you will separate for a pre-arranged length of time – anything from five minutes to half an hour. You must also agree that during this time you will not intrude on each other's space, and that you will return, as planned, to continue the discussion. This technique provides a cooling-off period, but with the assurance that you will not be left hanging with the issue unresolved.

However, there will also be times when you find yourself unexpectedly in a conflict situation, perhaps at work, or with a neighbour. In these instances, the first essential is to give yourself some emotional space. Rather than reacting, pause, and take a deep breath. This will relax your body, counteracting the stress response. Some people find it helps to also count to ten or recite the Lord's Prayer. You must then use these moments to consider your words, and how you can defuse the situation. Later, you might also need to find ways of safely giving vent to your feelings.

Release the Tension

If you have to suppress anger, and there is no outlet, it expands, like steam in a kettle with the vents blocked that has been left on a hot stove. Challenging your faulty thinking, or 'hot thoughts', is like taking the kettle off the stove, preventing an explosion. However, this is not always easy to do, and it takes time. So, meanwhile, you need to unblock the vents and let the steam out.

Since anger is a form of energy, which like any other form cannot be destroyed, only converted, it helps to do something physical – run round the block, scrub a floor, chop wood, pummel bread dough, throw soft, unbreakable items onto a bed.... Some people find a punch bag helpful, or a work-out in the gym, although this last is only useful if you can delay your need to let off steam. Others have found that writing a letter they have no intention of sending helps to release pent-up feelings. But

54

whatever you do, remember the golden rule: that you do nothing that will hurt yourself, other people or property. Also bear in mind that generally anger creates anger. These suggestions are first-aid measures only, intended to help you through the immediate crisis. They are not long-term methods of coping.

For more permanent ways of releasing tension, you need to have some regular physical activity – especially important if you tend to live a sedentary life. Physical exercise not only relieves stress, it also increases the number of circulating endorphins, which are known to lift mood. Walking or swimming are particularly beneficial, as is dancing; also any aggressive sport, such as rugby, football or squash. An active sex life within a committed and loving relationship will also help keep anger at bay, as well as improving your sense of well-being. If you have a physical disability that prevents vigorous activity, you will need to release your tension in small ways: clenching and unclenching your hands, verbalising your feelings, shouting, crying or laughing. A sense of humour is a great asset. And, since anger can accumulate in the body, a regular massage will not only relax your muscles, but also assist in releasing blocked emotions. When you have installed a permanent safely valve that keeps anger within normal bounds, you will then be in a better condition to begin addressing the cause.

Address the Cause

If your anger is primarily about global or environmental issues, rather than anything personal, then, instead of impotently raging against wrong and injustice, do something about it: get involved, perhaps with a political organisation or local group that is actively trying to protect the countryside or wildlife. You cannot save the world, but you can do something to bring about positive change in your own locality, and one that can have far wider repercussions.

If anger has built up because of a difficult relationship, then, where possible, you must confront the person who has angered you, not with the intention of letting off steam, but in order to improve the relationship. However, there are times when it is unwise to challenge someone who has wronged you, either because they wouldn't be able to handle it, or because they would become violent. In these cases, you can only confront the offender in your mind, work through the hurt and anger, and forgive. The same applies if you are in a relationship with someone who keeps on hurting you. You don't have to persist in trying to make things right. Rather, you need to question why you keep on exposing yourself to abuse, and start protecting yourself. Sometimes, addressing the cause means ending a relationship, reducing contact with relatives, getting out of an abusive church, or changing an unsatisfactory job.

You cannot, of course, escape from yourself. So if your anger is directed inwards, first, forgive yourself for any wrongs you actually have committed; and, while acknowledging the parts of yourself that you like, set about changing those aspects of yourself you don't like. And don't be so down on yourself, or so proud, that you cannot seek specialist assistance. You might, for instance, need help with spiritual issues, weight problems, drug or alcohol dependence, poor parenting skills, or emotional difficulties.

Whatever your problem, you can discover what help is available through your GP practice, library, Yellow Pages, or online. If you need counselling, and there is a counsellor attached to your doctor's surgery, then you can usually have six to eight sessions on the NHS. You can also locate a private counsellor or psychotherapist through the Association of Christian Counsellors (ACC), the British Association for Counselling and Psycho-therapy (BACP), or the UK Council for Psychotherapy (UKCP). But before investing your time and money, find out how the practitioner works. A cognitive behavioural therapist will focus on the here and now, helping you with such things as anger management, and any current issues you are struggling with; whereas a psychodynamic counsellor or psychotherapist, and to a lesser extent a person-centred counsellor, will also look at underlying causes, and help bring about the healing of old wounds.

But whatever the source of your anger, and however you choose to deal with it, you also need to acquire some coping skills, so that anger doesn't build up in the first place. Of particular importance are learning how to be assertive, how to deal with conflict, and how to relax.

LEARN SOME COPING SKILLS

Learn how to be Assertive.

If you have difficulty with assertiveness, the first step is to ask yourself why. Some common reasons for non-assertive, or passive, behaviour are fear of disapproval, fear of rejection and fear of retaliation. Or perhaps you mistakenly think that you should never deny any request, however unreasonable or persistent, whether for your time, money or labour. But setting boundaries is essential for your own well-being and self-respect, as well as for others. Without boundaries you will be walked over, trampled on, and depleted of energy, and you will end up being of no use to anyone. Moreover, you will not be helping permanently needy people develop their own sense of autonomy.

When you are non-assertive, you are in a lose-win situation: you lose, the other person wins. With this, you may avoid conflict, but your needs are not met, resulting in damaged self-esteem, disappointment in self, and accumulated anger. Passive verbal behaviour is characterised by rambling statements, hesitant, apologetic speech, and pleading, whiny or giggly tone. You are likely to also have a slumped body and bowed head, with shifting of weight, wringing hands, biting lip or other nervous gestures, and downcast, averted or tearful eyes.

If, on the other hand, you tend to be aggressive, you are in a win-lose situation. You win, but the other person loses. However, even if you get your way, you will damage your own integrity, and create anger and resentment in the other, who may start avoiding you, or seek revenge. Aggressive behaviour includes use of threats, put-downs, sarcasm, accusations, judgemental statements, and manipulation. Your tone of voice will probably be raised, or mocking, and you will tend to lean forward, with stiff posture, clenched hands, finger pointing, and glaring, narrowed eyes.

However, when you are assertive, you are in a win-win

situation. You stand up for your rights without undermining the rights of others. You will generally achieve your goals, but even if you don't, you will feel self-respecting and confident. Assertive behaviour is characterised by relaxed posture, standing firmly on two feet with hands loosely at your side. Eye contact is direct but not staring, expression pleasant, and your voice strong, steady and firm.

You might want to start rehearsing these assertive behaviours in front of a mirror. Then, practice saying 'no' to someone you trust and feel safe with before you face more threatening situations, like expressing dissatisfaction with a product or work issue, saying 'no' to salespeople, or voicing your opinions in a group setting. The times when you most need to be assertive are when you are being drained and need to re-charge your own batteries; when others are being excessively demanding, intrusive, manipulative or controlling; or when a child needs firm boundaries in order to feel safe. Most people will respect your boundaries, but some will continue to ignore them. A few might get angry and try to beat them down, in which case you also need to be able to deal with conflict.

Learn how to Deal with Conflict

There are basically four ways in which you can mishandle conflict, all of which create or increase anger. The first is to simply avoid it. This might seem like a way of also avoiding anger but, like passivity, it lowers your opinion of yourself, and will discredit you in the eyes of the other. And since the matter is not dealt with, you will continue to feel frustrated or annoyed. On the other hand, you can inflame the situation through exaggerating the problem or your feelings about it. A third dysfunctional method is escalation: moving from the issue, to the personal to the relationship. For example, if the conflict is about who is going to wash up (the issue), you may start getting personal – "You are a lazy slob!" – and end up questioning the relationship: "I don't know why I stay with you." Or you can mismanage conflict through 'dirty fighting'. Examples include choosing a bad time, bringing up past issues or unrelated current ones, listing faults or grievances, mind reading, pulling rank, or over-generalising: using words like 'always' or 'never'. Cross-complaining – responding to every complaint with one of your own – can keep the conflict going indefinitely.

While thinking about ways in which you might be causing or intensifying arguments, reflect also on your typical response. Do you tend to withdraw from the conflict as soon as you feel threatened, or give in to keep the peace? Do you look for a compromise, or feel that you have to win at all costs? Or, do you seek to resolve the situation?

In order to resolve conflict, first select an appropriate time, and avoid walking out during an argument, unless you have agreed beforehand to 'Time-out'. Then, being concise, define the problem as you see it and deal only with the issue specified, avoiding exaggeration, escalation and any dirty fighting. Listen carefully to the other, agree where possible, and try to understand the other's viewpoint, using empathic statements like, "I can see your point, but..." It helps also to use 'I' rather than 'you' statements. For example, "I get upset when you do that," not, "You really make me mad." With 'I' statements you are taking responsibility for your own feelings, and not accusing the other. When, in addition, you can identify and admit your own contribution to the problem, the other is more likely to cooperate.

If you are unable to resolve an issue, and compromise is not the answer, you can choose the gift principle. With this, you meet the other person, not halfway, but all the way. This is not yielding since you have actively chosen to give the other what he or she wants, not to end the argument, but as an expression of love. And this will be easier to do if you can first learn to love yourself. This involves knowing, respecting and caring for yourself, and taking responsibility for your own needs, including the need for rest and relaxation.

Learn to Rest and Relax

To rest means to abstain from work or exertion. If you are quickly aroused to anger, it could be because you drive yourself, trying to achieve more and more in increasingly less time. This tendency may have arisen in childhood, perhaps to win a parent's love and approval, or to compensate for some deficiency, real or imagined. Often, there is an internalised parental voice telling you that you can't sit down until a job is finished, or you're not allowed to go out while there's still housework to do. But rest is essential, and as long as your house or workplace isn't neglected, nothing dire is going to happen; rather, the opposite. When you listen to your body's needs, and stop when necessary, or do something different, you can resume your work with renewed energy.

As well as your body, you also need to rest your mind and soul. The mind can be rested through doing something that uses a different part of the brain. So, for example, if you work with accounts, try resting the logical side of the brain by stretching the more creative side, perhaps through painting or composing poetry. If your daytime job involves writing, designing, or working with people, then do something that requires memorising sequences, such as dancing. You can also rest your mind through simply switching off and allowing it to wander, or through reflection or meditation. This will also rest your soul and spirit, especially if you meditate on God and the beauty of his creation. And remember, God has set a principle of one day's rest to every six days' work.

It is also essential that you also learn to relax, which means reducing tension. Begin by thinking about something that makes you angry, and note the physical sensations. Now think about something relaxing – a garden or woodland, a sunny beach, or the sea lapping onto the shore – and notice the difference. Also make a point of doing things that are relaxing for you, like walking or gardening. And bring some more fun into your life. The more you can keep your muscular tension within normal limits, the less easily you will be provoked to anger, and the easier it will be to manage.

In addition, you can practice some relaxation exercises. Any form of relaxation activates the parasympathetic nervous system, which is part of the body's homeostatic device: it lowers blood pressure and pulse rate, and makes you less rigid and tense. Quickie relaxation takes only a few minutes, and can be practiced in odd moments throughout the day. First, sit comfortably, loosen your clothing, close your eyes and take three deep breaths through your nose, exhaling slowly through the mouth. Then, breathing normally, slowly stretch, at the same time tightening your entire body. Then let yourself go limp and, after about ten seconds, conclude the exercise by taking three more deep breaths. When you tighten the muscles first, the relaxation is deeper, as a pendulum swings more to the left if you first pull it to the right. Progressive relaxation takes longer as you tighten and relax each muscle group in turn, beginning with your toes and working up to your head.

Learning to rest and relax is particularly important if you have a high base anger level, perhaps because of unresolved experience of wrong, injustice or pain. Misuse of any kind, especially if it occurred in childhood, causes such extensive damage that it hinders any attempt to implement changes, or deal with the normal frustrations of life. So although it helps to acquire some anger management techniques, it is not enough. In order to grow into wholeness, and develop a deep sense of inner calm, you have to find healing for past injuries, improve your current lifestyle, and work at enhancing all aspects of yourself – heart, mind, body, soul and spirit.

5

GROWING BEYOND ANGER

WORK THROUGH PAST TRAUMAS

Acknowledge the Facts

When there is a persistent anger problem, it is usually because of unresolved injuries from the past. In this case, before you can move on, you have to go back, locate the original trauma and work through the pain and anger. 'Working through' means first of all facing the reality of the harm done to you, and putting the responsibility where it belongs – not in order to blame or condemn, but so that you can get in touch with and process your true feelings, and ultimately forgive.

You then need to talk about your painful experiences – or express them through writing, perhaps in the form of a journal, autobiographical sketches or poetry. Putting vague or fragmented thoughts into words is releasing. It also gives them shape and substance, making it easier to understand them and invest them with meaning. Moreover, as you relate the facts as you remember them, a picture will build up that will enable you to see more clearly the reasons for your anger, and any dysfunctional patterns of behaviour. The more insight you have, the more you will be able to move beyond anger, rather than simply learning how to control it.

Understanding a deep-rooted anger problem might be more difficult if your childhood was basically happy. However, as you start telling your story, you will probably discover that your anger comes from a combination of painful circumstances that you have discounted or minimised. Or you might have unknowingly stored up anger because your parents, though well intentioned, were unable to meet your emotional needs. It is harder to recognise sins of omission than commission, especially if you have falsely convinced yourself that you cannot miss what you have never had. Children need to be loved and nurtured, to be listened to and understood, and to feel safe. And if parents, for whatever reason, failed to provide these essential requirements, it creates a gap in the child's psyche, making it harder to cope with the normal ups and downs of life. And inevitably, it creates great anger. This, along with any other hidden emotion, has to come to the surface before it can be processed.

Allow Feelings to Surface

As well as acknowledging the facts of past wrongs, it is essential that you also recognise and reconnect with the feelings. At first, as you begin to disclose experiences of trauma, abuse or neglect, it might feel as if you are talking about someone else. This dissociation is commonly used as a defence, in order to avoid painful emotions. But defences do not eliminate feelings; they only block them, forcing them out in other, more destructive ways – psychosomatic symptoms, depression, anxiety states, self-harm, or explosive rages that damage others. It is for this reason that merely recalling the feelings is not enough; you also have to feel them, and reclaim them as your own.

Feelings, however, cannot be forced. They will surface at their own speed, when you are ready for them to do so. And since you are no longer in the hurtful situation, they will be experienced in a milder, more manageable form. Nevertheless, you will still need to provide them with some outlet. As with narrating the facts of past hurts, talking about your feelings to another, who can respond appropriately with empathy and understanding, is the best option. But you can also express them through writing, music, dance, or any art form, such as painting or sculpture. And of course, you can talk about your hurt and anger to God. This is especially important if you are angry with God. But you must be truthful. If you try to spiritualise the problem, or rationalise it away, perhaps telling yourself that you couldn't possibly be angry with a loving and perfect heavenly Father, then he cannot give you the help and reassurance you need, just as an earthly father cannot help a hurt and angry child who refuses to admit that there is anything wrong.

It is only as you remove your mask, reveal your true self and honestly admit your feelings, that God can come alongside and help you use your emotions as he intended. Jesus said, "...the truth [reality] will set you free".[8] And this means being truthful about who you are really angry with, and about any displacement onto the wrong person or thing. Emotional wounds cannot heal if you are disclaiming them, confusing them, or making them worse through self-abuse or neglect. Neither can they heal if you have allowed your anger to turn to bitterness or wrath because of a refusal to forgive.

Work at Forgiveness

Forgiveness, it has been noted, does not mean that you accept the wrong that has been done to you. Neither does it mean making excuses for the perpetrators, or putting yourself back in an abusive situation. It is also not the same as reconciliation, although forgiveness can and often does lead to the re-establishment of a severed relationship. Forgiveness is for something that is unacceptable, for behaviour that should not be condoned or tolerated. It can be defined as the letting go of the desire for revenge or restitution. So, if you are still seeking revenge, hoping that those who hurt you will suffer, or looking for an apology or some form of compensation, then you have not yet forgiven.

Forgiveness is a process, and it begins with accepting and acknowledging the fact that you have been injured, and admitting the full extent of the injury. Sometimes, however, forgiveness occurs in stages, or at different levels, because you can only forgive to the extent that you are aware of the wrong done to you. Also, if the injury is very great, as for instance if you have been robbed of a childhood, you might not be able to forgive all at once. It may help to think of the Bible story of the unmerciful servant, which describes forgiveness in monetary terms.

A servant who had been found guilty of embezzlement, owed the king millions of pounds, which he couldn't possibly repay. And, threatened with dire punishment for himself and family, he pleaded with the king – who represents God – to forgive the debt, which the king agreed to do. But then, the servant met a fellow worker who owed him a very small amount, about ten pounds. And when he couldn't pay, the unmerciful servant had him thrown into prison. When the king heard about it he was very angry, and because his servant would not forgive his fellow the small debt, the king refused to forgive him the enormous one, and demanded full repayment.

When you don't forgive, it's like sending out a bill every month, with threats or demands for repayment, to someone whose unpaid debt has robbed you of emotional health or success, severely hindering the business of living. And with every bill, and every failure to pay, your anger increases. However, when you forgive, through writing across the bill, 'Paid in Full,' you no longer waste time and effort over something that can never be recovered. So you can channel your energies into re-building your life. You might at times feel sad, regretful and annoyed when you consider what you have lost, but without the constant drain of trying to re-coup your losses, you can focus more on improving the present, and making new and exciting plans for the future.

ENHANCE CURRENT RELATIONSHIPS

Live in Harmony with Yourself

As you work through past wrongs, facing the reality of any mistreatment and voicing your true feelings, you will discover, amongst other things, that you are less inclined to turn your anger inwards. However, you will still need to constantly assess the way you treat yourself, and check any urges to self-harm, physical or psychological. When there has been abuse or neglect in childhood, whether from family, school or peers, there is a tendency to be harsh with oneself, or to ignore one's own needs, perhaps not even to recognise them; to become, in fact, one's own worst enemy. But we are told to love our neighbour as ourselves,[9] not better than or instead of ourselves. Read 1 Corinthians 13, and apply this to yourself. How patient are you with yourself, how kind, how forgiving, and how true to yourself?

As you learn to be a good parent to yourself, nurturing, protecting and enriching yourself, your self-esteem will start improving. Self-esteem is not the same as selfishness or self-interest, and it is not entirely dependent on your performance or achievements. It is something much deeper, and involves the development of all aspects of the self. It also means being real: recognising and acknowledging your strengths and abilities, as well as your weaknesses.

With a healthy self-esteem you will be more creative and productive, and you will achieve results, but without pressuring yourself. You will be able to deal with conflict, and handle constructive criticism without going on the defensive, attacking, or plunging into despair; while your inner security will enable you to delegate, and keep you from acting with unwarranted jealousy and rage at any perceived rejection or put down. You will not need to fight to win recognition or power, or constantly struggle to beat deadlines. And you will not need to make others conform to your own ideas and wishes. Instead, you will be more patient with their shortcomings, and be able to stand back and allow them to develop in their own time and way. When you esteem yourself, it is easier to esteem and respect others.

Live Peaceably with Others

Living in harmony with yourself is a vital requisite for living peaceably with others. And the more you get to know and love yourself, the more you will be able to empathise: to put yourself in someone else's shoes and imagine how they might be feeling. You will also be able to identify with those who have been through similar experiences, but without getting over-involved, and without the compulsion to care for others in order to vicariously meet your own needs. You will therefore be in less danger of becoming emotionally exhausted and resentful, and you will be able to respond to the real needs of others, as opposed to what you think they need.

However, it takes two to form a relationship, and it is not always possible to live peaceably with another. In this case, the important thing to remember is that your anger, or lack of it, is not dependent on someone else's feelings or behaviour. If someone is angry with you, begin by allowing it, accepting this as a normal human emotion. If their anger is excessive, don't allow yourself to be intimidated, and don't change your behaviour in order to appease the other. Instead, apply the principles for managing conflict, reminding yourself that you don't have to get angry to get your point across. It is a truism that if you have authority you don't need to shout. This is particularly true when it comes to dealing with children.

But whether you are trying to connect with young people or other adults, you can only live in harmony with them if, besides tuning into them – as far as they will allow – you enable them to see the real you. You have to start removing your defences. If you have a tendency to keep others at arm's length, then you will need to work at receiving love as well as giving it. Begin by reflecting on the fact that, when you reject others' offerings of appreciation, praise and encouragement, emotional support or practical help, you are actually rejecting them. There will, of course, be times when you will need to distance yourself. Living in harmony with others does not mean being gullible. But as you learn to discriminate, you will find it easier to be open, to experience the interchange of love, and to form deep and lasting relationships.

Live at one with Creation
The more you are able to live at peace with yourself and others, the more you will connect with the entire created world.

And conversely, the more you fulfil your God-given task to care for and protect the environment, the deeper will be your sense of inner harmony. But while this peace process will occur naturally as the inner turmoil lessens, you can accelerate it through actively thinking about the world around you and how you are treating it, and by determining to use your anger in constructive ways: to bring healing and health where there has been damage and disease.

Throughout history there have been periods when people have been very aware of the deep connection we have with the animal and plant world, and our responsibility towards it. And in this day and age there is, thankfully, a growing recognition (or re-knowing) of a truth that has existed from the beginning of time. Adam was given authority over all living things, and the task of naming them – which involves knowing – and caring for them. Authority does not mean domination, and neither does it mean that we can use nature in any way we want. Anger, you will recall, is a drive to life. So, as you concern yourself more with the life of our planet, you will be using your anger in positive ways, to bring peace and harmony. You will also benefit yourself as consequently you develop a greater sense of meaning and purpose, and enhance your spiritual awareness.

Experience the Peace of God

If you have experienced mistreatment in the past, and especially if you have been hurt by a religious leader or church, you may have displaced your anger onto God, making him an enemy instead of the friend he wants to be. You may even have denied his existence or, while shutting down painful emotions, also silenced the divinity within: that inner voice that tells us there is something greater than ourselves and the material world around us. But in order to fully develop as human beings, we have to get in touch with the spiritual aspect of ourselves. So, as you work through any painful experiences, ask yourself if you are transferring onto all believers, or God himself, the negative attributes of one person or group of people who have hurt you. And, in addition to searching the Scriptures, ask God to show you what he is really like.

We have been promised that if we seek we shall find.[10] But it is important that, as you search, you stay within the boundaries God has set for our protection. This basically excludes anything that would involve you in the occult, which means 'secret'. God is a God of light, not darkness: he brings all things out into the open. He is also a God of love. So don't be deceived by anyone who claims to be acting in God's name, yet sets out to maim and destroy. Your best starting point for discovering the true character of God is the Gospels, which describe the birth, life and death of Christ. For Jesus said, "Anyone who has seen me has seen the Father".[11] You can also get to know God through prayer, which is meant to be a two-way communication, or through the example of godly people: those who demonstrate love and compassion, who do not judge and condemn, but allow you to question and doubt, to work through your hurt and turmoil and experience the peace of God in your own time and your own way.

As you start living more in harmony with yourself, other people, creation and the Creator, you will be able to look forward with hope. Although, in this world, there will always be wrong, injustice and pain, these will no longer overwhelm you, causing you to rail impotently against evil. Instead you will be able to use your anger to bring about lasting and beneficial change, not just in yourself, but also in the world around you.

MAKE CHANGES FOR THE FUTURE

Change Yourself

Change always has to begin with yourself. But don't try to do everything at once. While it is essential to develop all five aspects of the self – heart, mind, body, soul and spirit – begin by thinking about your areas of particular difficulty, and start with these. Is it the social self (heart) that causes you the most problems? If so, then think of ways in which you can improve relationships. Maybe you have gravitated towards friends who manipulate and control, or needy, demanding friends who always take and give nothing in return. Or perhaps your anger has kept people at a distance and you've tended to be a loner. In order to make friends you have to be friendly. So make the first move. Start going to places where you will meet new people, invite them for coffee, re-contact old friends with whom you've lost touch. And be patient with yourself. Friends are not made overnight.

But perhaps, rather than your social life, it is your mind you have neglected. In that case, look for ways to exercise your brain. Read more widely, attend lectures, or join a group with shared interests, such as history or writing, or go back to college. You can also visit art galleries, exhibitions, museums, or go to plays and concerts. We are meant to use our minds, and develop their full potential, through exploring God's Word and his works in creation.

We are also meant to take care of our bodies, keeping them as healthy and attractive as possible. If it is your body image you are struggling with, or you are angry at an illness or disability, then rather than bemoaning your lot, do something about it. Turn your anger into a determination to lose weight, stop drinking to excess or smoking, increase mobility, or find new ways of functioning.

Your soul can be enhanced through exposing yourself to love, beauty and truth, those virtues on which it thrives. Give yourself space to reflect and meditate, and time to stand and stare, enjoying this beautiful world God has created. Take yourself into the country or seaside, wander through gardens or woodlands, and use all five senses to absorb the wonders of nature. Not only will this enrich your soul, it will also aid the development of your spirit, so you will have a greater sense of connection with God. You will also discover that you cannot bask in beauty and, at the same time, be angry.

The many ways in which you can enhance all aspects of yourself are explored more fully in the book, *Self-Esteem, the Way of Humility*. Also discussed is the topic of self-identity. You cannot esteem yourself if you don't know who you are. And you cannot know who you are if you are being controlled or coerced by another, or driving yourself unnecessarily. Self-discovery occurs in the context of play, which involves freedom and spontaneity, and the ability to relax and have fun. And this, of course, applies to others as well as yourself.

Change Society

You cannot change another person, because others too have to be free to develop in their own time and way. But what you can do is act as a role model, and create a loving and safe environment in which change can take place. So as you set about making a better future for yourself, your family and society as a whole, begin by thinking of ways in which you can make the atmosphere at home more conducive to peace and harmony, focusing especially on your own behaviours. And consider any practical solutions, such as re-organising meal times, arranging family outings, or creating some physical space where it is possible to relax and unwind. If you live in a threatening and hostile neighbourhood, then use your anger to put a stop to any harassment: get together with like-minded neighbours, determine on a plan of action, and carry it through. You do not have to keep on being a helpless victim.

Further afield, there are things you can do to change society. But be realistic. Consider your current commitments, the time you have available, and your age and state of health. But even if you can't do much practically, there are other ways of contributing to society's needs, perhaps financially, or through providing support and encouragement. If you do have time on your hands, maybe volunteer work would give you an added interest, as well as enabling you to do something about issues that anger you. There is a wide variety of work to choose from, such as charity shops, children's work, caring for the elderly, helping at your local school, or perhaps looking after sick or injured animals, getting involved with young people or joining a protest group. If you don't feel that any of these are for you, then perhaps you could perform a valuable function in the background, dealing with accounts or correspondence, organising or liaising.

But whatever you do, remember the maxim that, however you channel your anger, you do nothing that harms yourself, other people or property. When fighting for the rights of a minority group, animals, etc., you must do this assertively – not aggressively – respecting the rights of others. You cannot prevent wrong by doing wrong. And you cannot bring about justice through treating others unjustly, or reduce pain by causing pain. This principle also applies when you seek to change the environment.

Change the Environment

If you are angry about the way our planet is being abused, then, as with changing society, use your anger in constructive ways, to build up, restore, protect and preserve. But here too you will need to be realistic, while not discounting any contribution you can make to the welfare of our planet, no matter how small. Again, begin at home, perhaps thinking of ways you can better manage your own part of the environment. Do you, for example, waste electricity, throw away excessive amounts of food, or make poor use of natural resources? Sometimes only a few minor adjustments can make a considerable difference. In your garden, you can contribute to the planet's well-being through planting shrubs and flowers that will attract insects, or putting seeds out for the birds, especially over the winter months. If you own a large plot of land or farm, consider going organic, re-planting hedgerows and leaving spaces for birds to nest and rear their young, and for wildlife to thrive.

While working on your own environment, also consider the larger picture. You might want to send money to organisations that plant trees or provide domestic animals for people who are struggling to support themselves. Or get involved with a local environmental group, perhaps caring for trees, beaches or endangered species. Here, as with social concerns, you might prefer to simply add your voice to the many others now rising up in protest, or work indirectly doing essential clerical work, making tea, or helping with maintenance.

With everything you do to change yourself or the world in which you live, you are working off your anger, doing something positive for the here and now, and leaving a precious legacy for future generations. Anyone can lash out, yell and scream, or endlessly complain about prevailing conditions. But it takes real power to right wrongs, resolve injustice, bring healing to sick minds and bodies, and hope where there is despair.

LOOK FORWARD WITH HOPE

Righting Wrongs

Learning some anger management techniques is relatively easy. But to grow beyond anger takes time and a lot of hard work, especially if you have a backlog of anger resulting from childhood traumas. And it involves, not only learning how to keep anger in check, but understanding and developing all aspects of yourself, making use of the whole range of emotions, and finding creative ways of using your anger constructively. Maybe you have been wronged, but rather than adding to it, by allowing bitterness or wrath to take over, use your anger to right wrongs.

Anger can be used in so many useful ways. It can, for instance, provide the energy needed to perform routine tasks, handle emergencies and overcome disappointments, enabling you to either try again or attempt something new. Anger can be used to promote personal growth and development and enhance relationships. It can challenge immorality, fight corruption, bring about reforms, stop wars, and reverse the destruction of our planet. And anger can be used to bring justice where there has been false dealing, discrimination and inequality.

Bringing Justice

If you have been treated unjustly, then instead of lashing out in anger, creating yet more injustice, turn your experiences around, so that good can come from evil. That way, you are actually getting your revenge, but in a positive way. Your ability to rise above your misfortunes, to develop and grow and achieve your ambitions, demonstrates that those who maligned or misjudged you have failed. And even if they are not aware of your success, *you* will know; and there will be a sense of triumph as you master your own baser nature and come through with your integrity intact.

As with righting wrongs, anger that is used to fight injustice can achieve great things – above and beyond your own personal concerns. It can remodel businesses, reform churches, and restructure social organisations. It can stop bullying in schools, prevent perpetrators of neighbourhood crime getting the upper hand, put a halt to victimisation of minority groups, and change unjust laws that protect the guilty, penalise the innocent, and burden the poor and needy. When anger is used, not to wreak vengeance, but to put a stop to evil, it also prevents a lot of unnecessary suffering.

Relieving Suffering

When you are hurt, the natural tendency is to want to hurt in return. But when, instead, you use your anger to soothe pain and bring healing and health, you are demonstrating real power. And here again, anger has many uses. It can, for instance, provide the energy needed to fight cancer or care for a sick relative. It can nurse abused or neglected animals back to health, rescue children from lives of exploitation and misery, ensure the elderly are treated with care and respect, stop torture, and bind up the wounds of those who have suffered, physically and emotionally.

When you use anger to right wrongs, bring justice and alleviate pain and suffering, then, like John, the Son of Thunder, you are combining anger with love. The Bible tells us that God is love; but also that he, like humans, is angry every day when he sees wrong, injustice and pain. The anger of God is actually mentioned 375 times. But anger and love are not incompatible. On the contrary, they go together. And it is when the two are joined that anger can be used creatively, to bring life, peace and prosperity. This is also what Naomi discovered. Her love for her daughter-in-law kept her from becoming bitter and twisted as she grieved the loss of her husband and sons. And it was love and respect that enabled Elihu to use his anger to challenge false thinking, making it possible for Job to turn his fortunes around. And as you start merging anger with love, you will find that deep within you is a growing sense of calm.

Developing an Inner Calm

Ultimately, it is only as you learn to love, thereby finding peace with God, who is love, that you can develop that deep sense of inner calm that endures however hurt and angry you are at the evil that exists in today's world. So, as you practice harnessing your anger, and using it in positive ways, also learn how to love –

to love yourself, your neighbour, this beautiful planet of ours, and our Creator God.

With love and anger combined, you can have a powerful impact on the world around you. Anger that has been channelled in love can bring peace and happiness where there has been damage and despair; it can promote truth and freedom where there has been deceit and bondage; and it can create beauty and enjoyment where there has been suffering and sorrow. Anger can climb the highest mountain, plumb the deepest ocean, and cross the widest desert. Anger can achieve the impossible.

Endnotes

1	Psalms 7: 11
2	Ruth 1: 16-17
3	Matthew 27: 56
4	Mark 16: 1
5	John 19: 25
6	Ephesians 4: 26
7	Proverbs 15: 1
8	John 8: 32
9	Mark 12: 33
10	Matthew 7: 7
11	John 14: 9

The Grobook Series by Jennifer Minney

BEYOND DEPRESSION: GROWING INTO LIGHT
ISBN: 0-9538446-3-3

BEYOND STRESS: GROWING INTO SERENITY
ISBN: 0-9538446-4-1

BEYOND FEAR: GROWING INTO FAITH
ISBN: 0-9538446-5-X   **All titles £3.50**

Jennifer Minney, an experienced counsellor, SRN and SCM, with a BA (Summa cum Laude) in Psychology and a Bible College Diploma with Distinction, has combined medical and psychological knowledge with biblical truths to produce a series of books on some common emotional problems that hinder personal growth and development.

Using Bible characters as case studies, each book discusses causes, signs and symptoms, and gives practical suggestions for overcoming the immediate effects. The reader is also helped to understand and change dysfunctional patterns of thinking and behaviour: to move beyond the problem towards spiritual and psychological wholeness.

The still all-too-common belief that depression, stress and fear are emotions never experienced by 'real' Christians must cause deep pain to lovely Christian people who find themselves travelling through dark, fraught or worrying valleys simply because they, like the rest of humankind, are mortal. So it is a joy to recommend these three titles, written by an ACW member who is also a qualified and experienced counsellor.

The books are professionally presented, all in a manageable 80 pages long. The tone is conversational and friendly, without becoming sloppy or losing the note of professional assurance. The anticipated experience for the reader is a healing journey into a confident future. These titles, as a set, would be a very valuable pastoral resource for any caring Christian.

                    The Association of Christian Writers

Also by Jennifer Minney

LIVING THROUGH GRIEF
ISBN: 0-9536446-6-8   32pp   **£2.50**

*This is an extremely useful little book for anybody going through
the pain of grief and also for those who need guidance on helping
the bereaved.... Heartily recommended.*
                              The Association of Christian Writers

*Delivers professional advice in an accessible and positive way.
Informative and helpful, in no way or patronising... with a broad
readability and distilled experience.*
                         The Association of Christian Counsellors

SELF-ESTEEM: THE WAY OF HUMILITY
ISBN: 0-9538446-2-5   144pp   **£5.95**

*The author is a qualified counsellor with years of experience in
both the Christian and secular sectors, but what makes her book
so valuable is that it is written by someone who also has a deep
and intelligent understanding of the Bible and distinction at
degree level in psychology. And she is a very fine writer. These
combined credentials shine through the text, giving the book a
dimension which sets it apart from the usual self-help book,
secular or Christian.*

*In a very clear way, the book achieves its purpose of helping
people escape from the tyranny of deep-rooted untruths about
themselves and about God which have robbed them of the
experience of receiving and giving love without hindrance in their
relationships with others, with God and with themselves.*
                              The Association of Christian Writers

*She looks at how we see ourselves, our need of love and
acceptance, our creativity and innate curiosity, the relationships
between body, mind and soul... I commend it.*
                         The Association of Christian Counsellors

WILL JESUS KICK MY BALL BACK?
ISBN 0-9538446-0-9   173pp   **£6.95**

The amazing story of an adoption that should have been impossible, and of an endearing, giggly child whom a neurologist had written off. It is also the story of the author's spiritual and psychological journey, from a background of abuse and rejection to a place of trust in God's goodness.

The book cannot help but be an uplifting read. Indeed, this reviewer was moved to tears by the poem that stands as a preface to the tale, and Jennifer Minney's honesty and sensitive writing evoke empathy and admiration throughout..... A lovely portrayal of the constantly metamorphosing relationship between parents, child and God. If you haven't read this book, you should.

The Association of Christian Writers

SONG OF CREATION
ISBN: 0-9538446-1-7   96pp   **£4.50**

An unusual and though-provoking anthology based on the seven days of creation. The poems, which range from free verse to sonnets, celebrate life in all its varied forms. Many have a Celtic flavour and reflect on God's revelation of himself through creation. They also explore the creative process and seek a new understanding of our relationship with the entire created world.

All books available, post free, from:

**Silvertree Publishing
PO Box 2768
Yeovil
BA22 8XZ**

**Tel: 01935 862127
www.silvertreepublishing.co.uk**